MW00737134

Praise for *At Home in the World*

"For anyone who loves to explore diverse cultures, At Home in the World *will inspire your next journey. Dorothy Conlon is a true world citizen who gets personally involved wherever she goes, making her stories real and passionate. Her trips are not vacations but in-depth travel immersions where she combines living, working and participating in local life. I admire Dorothy's courage as a traveler and wisdom as a story teller. This is an inspiring and terrific book!"*

— Leslie Butterfield, Ph.D.
Corporate Communications Consultant

"Dorothy Conlon is one of those irrepressible can-do spirits whose travel accounts arouse our own nostalgia for far-off places."

— Donald Y. Gilmore,
Retired Foreign Service Officer

"Dorothy's description of her many travels delights all the senses. I could smell and taste the spicy Indian foods, feel my leg muscles grow tired trekking the hilly country in Central America, hear the lovely cadence of Spanish and Mayan dialects, as well as see not only the diverse topography but also the beauty of people in their unique world cultures. Conlon moves between history, geography, and personal narrative in a seamless way that is sure to please her readers and have them planning adventures of their own."

— J. Lynn McBrien, Ph.D.
Assistant Professor of Education,
University of South Florida

For Georgiana,

Travel vicariously with me!

AT HOME IN THE WORLD

Memoirs of a Traveling Woman

by Dorothy S. Conlon

Dorothy Conlon

PublishAmerica
Baltimore

© 2007 by Dorothy S. Conlon.
All rights reserved. No part of this book may be reproduced, stored in a retrieval system or transmitted in any form or by any means without the prior written permission of the publishers, except by a reviewer who may quote brief passages in a review to be printed in a newspaper, magazine or journal.

First printing

At the specific preference of the author, PublishAmerica allowed this work to remain exactly as the author intended, verbatim, without editorial input.

ISBN: 1-4137-9160-3
PUBLISHED BY PUBLISHAMERICA, LLLP
www.publishamerica.com
Baltimore

Printed in the United States of America

DEDICATION

TO THE EVER VIBRANT MEMORY OF

NED, BRUCE AND BRAD CONLON

ACKNOWLEDGMENTS

My deepest gratitude goes to Sarah Seidman, without whose warm encouragement and professional editing skill, these travel stories would still languish in a bottomless file drawer.

Equally professional assistance was contributed by Joy Erickson, who volunteered to be my graphics consultant. Her creativity in working with my color slides has added greatly to the total impact of this project.

Many other friends have held my hand as I navigated the mysteries of producing this book. Thanks.

"As the traveler who has once been from home is wiser...so a knowledge of one other culture should sharpen our ability to scrutinize more steadily, to appreciate more lovingly our own."
—*Margaret Mead*

Tunisia

Bhutan

India

Thailand   Vietnam

Japan

Tanzania

River in
Zimbabwe

Namibia

Kangaroo Island
South Australia

Contents

INTRODUCTION

When our teenaged son Brad was at boarding school in the Palani Hills of South India, he started writing a journal.

Ever since I was in 3rd or 4th grade people have been telling me I should start a record of happenings because my life was bound to be interesting, maybe not for me but for other Americans who have not spent their whole lives traveling around the world. At first I thought it was a waste of time. Then I began to realize that my experiences had been quite different from other peoples, but I wasn't inspired enough to get down to writing what happened to me.

Finally, I've come to the conclusion that it doesn't really matter whether others would find my experiences interesting or not, but for myself they would be invaluable, so I started a diary. Besides just experiences, I want to record feelings, thoughts, and ideas. In other words it should not only show the pattern of my actions, but also the pattern of my mind. I've already let 16 years escape recording, but hopefully my mind will still retain it.

Alas, Brad's journaling—all five books of it—ended up with far more details of what he had to eat and how often he and his girlfriend got together than of the "feelings, thoughts and ideas" that he had vowed to record.

Now, here I am at age eighty, compiling not the story of my life, but selected adventures and excursions from a lifetime of foreign living and travel. Like Brad, I hope they reveal "the pattern of my mind" as well as insights into the far lands I have experienced. My life—like many—has been a mosaic including great blessings as well as great sorrows.

From my earliest childhood in a missionary family in Japan, I somehow knew I was meant to be a world citizen. As an adult I spent twenty-five great years living abroad, on assignments with the United States Foreign Service. Some of those two to five year stays were more difficult, some more fun, but all of them were enriching on one level or another.

The logical next step after my husband's retirement was to continue my traveling life in the form of short jaunts rather than long stays. During the next twelve years, accidents and illness took the lives of our two sons and eventually of my husband as well. I found it a welcome distraction from grief to indulge my unabated wanderlust. No longer anchored by family responsibilities, I was free to explore. The adaptability developed from all our moving around has made it easy for me to go journeying independently, even without the security of an employer and a formal work assignment.

Just because I wasn't heading off for a job doesn't mean that I haven't worked. Over the years I've participated in a dozen or more short-term projects under different auspices: English teaching, monitoring cheetahs or dolphins for scientific research, even laboring in construction. Volunteer travel—sometimes called service-learning—has proven to be an unexpected source of great delight and insight. Working right alongside the people of other countries inevitably broadens one's world view. And if local people have an image of the Ugly American, working and living together helps dispel that a bit. Volunteering abroad provides a very different perspective from what the tourist sees, and besides, it's fun.

Friends say that I'm brave to travel alone, and to such exotic places, but it doesn't seem that way to me. Anybody could do it, and without spending a fortune. In many places, solo adventures open up new doors for you, offering connections with the local people that you would never experience if you were part of a group or even traveling with a buddy. One of our sons taught me that long ago, and I can vouch for its truth. In an essay about travel, Joe Robinson once wrote "Something happens out there that cranks up the can-do spirit." To that I say "Amen."

The following episodes—a baker's dozen—relate just a few of my experiences from the past twenty-odd years, tales to whet your travel appetite and tempt you to go voyaging until you, too, feel "at home in the world."

INDIA Sri Meenakshi temple

CHAPTER 1

1984
MY LOVE AFFAIR WITH INDIA

I never expected to like India. In fact, I never wanted to go there, even when I joined the Foreign Service and had to promise to go anywhere in the world that I might be sent. In my inner soul I said to myself, "anywhere except India."

But now it's 1984. Not only did I live happily in India for five years in the 1970s, but I often feel the need to return. India has become a very important part of my life and of who I am today. What all has led to this transformation?

In the spring of 1971 our family of four was living in *Hong Kong* when my husband Ned was given a direct transfer to the American Consulate General in *Madras*—now called *Chennai*—in the southern Indian state of Tamil Nadu. It had looked for a while as though an assignment in *Washington* was inevitable, which none of us wanted just then. Our two boys were young teenagers and dead set against transferring to an American high school midway. So India it was, my stiff upper lip firmly in place.

Ned had to leave *Hong Kong* rather suddenly, before the boys' school year was finished. I followed about a month later with Bruce and Brad whose new school, a boarding school in the *Palani Hills* of South India, would be starting shortly. No summer vacation for them. But first, we had an unexpected overnight in *Calcutta*, of all places.

A last-minute message from Ned instructed us to spend the night in *Calcutta* instead of making a direct airport transfer to *Madras*. This was in the days of the Bangladeshi War, so security at DumDum Airport was tight. We were met not by an official US Consulate car but by a humble taxi sent by the Consulate—low profile, you know. No sooner had we three started on the long ride into the city, squished into the small black and yellow taxi, than the heavens opened. Rain teemed down while skeletal men pulling old-fashioned rickshaws jogged through deep water alongside the rutted roadway. What a dismal welcome to India. None of us was thrilled to be here. The next morning's taxi ride back out to the airport was in much cheerier sunshine, and our arrival in *Madras* was positively euphoric.

Not only was Ned there to meet us, but the roomy Consulate sedan whisked us the short distance to our spacious house where smiling servants were waiting to greet us with garlands of marigolds. The sun was bright; the garden was full of tall poinsettia bushes and topiary shrubs. Our new home was cool and comfortable, with polished terrazzo floors and ceiling fans. What a welcome. From that moment on, all of my preconceptions of India were blasted. The warmth of the South Indian people we soon met, the fascination of their ancient culture, the whole enticing laid-back atmosphere; I was totally bewitched.

In my early Foreign Service days, I would get antsy spending two whole years in any single place. After all, at that rate I wouldn't live long enough to see all the countries I wanted to around the globe. But India so charmed me that our five years there flew by. Before getting too involved in community life, I promptly started exploring this new—to me—huge country. I'll never forget my first foray, to the southwestern coastal state of Kerala, accompanied by another

Consulate wife. Lee also was new to India, young and as curious about our surroundings as I. People sometimes took her to be my daughter. What a variety of sights and experiences. We wandered the tight little streets of Jewtown in *Cochin* and stayed in a former maharajah's stately palace in *Kottayem*, sleeping under mosquito nets.

It was at the palace that I received a useful lesson in social customs. One of our few fellow diners at the long carved table was a handsome Indian businessman, probably not yet thirty. In his relaxed chattiness he raved about his wife; they were quite newly married. We Americans, of course, find the concept of arranged marriages mysterious and repugnant, so it was with some trepidation that I grew bold enough to ask if this was an arranged marriage. Surprised, he said, "Of course." Otherwise, how would he have found a wife, as colleges are segregated and open dating is rarely permitted. It turned out that his parents had presented several likely applicants to him over the course of the last few years. I pressed on. What, I queried, was so different or special about the girl he had finally chosen? He laughed as he said that probably they all would have been fine, but when this one came along, he was *ready* to be married. It was basically a matter of timing.

After drifting down the narrow backwaters in a ferryboat, observing vibrant river life all around us, Lee and I reached *Alleppey* in time for the annual "snakeboat" races. A little like Chinese dragon boats, these brightly painted long boats are manned by festooned crews of sixty or more men, well fed and well oiled. We were totally enveloped by the merry festival crowd.

During our entire trip we saw only the occasional foreigner. But we were not stared at, only greeted warmly by Indians from every walk of life. People of each town told us that we shouldn't go to the next place. It's so much nicer here, they always said. Everywhere were broad Arabian Sea beaches, coconut groves, *padi* fields, and royal estates. No wonder my appetite for Indian travel was whetted; no wonder that Kerala remains my favorite state in all of India. The only complaint I can conjure up is this: much as I love the varied flavors of Indian food, in Kerala the cloying taste of coconut oil overrides their wonderful pungent spices.

That was the first of my many trips within India. Often I traveled with Ned when he went on official business to *Bangalore* or *Hyderabad*. Other times I would find a willing travel partner usually from the Madras Consulate, and we would design a jaunt to temple towns such as *Jaipur* or *Ajanta* and *Ellora*, or to some unpronounceable destination that I had heard of, with the help of Matthew, the office travel expert. Of course India is so large that I still had a list of unexplored places I wanted to see when we finally left the country in 1976.

By this time Bruce, a gregarious nineteen-year-old, had finished high school and started college in *Washington, DC.* Ned was honored to give the commencement address when Brad, sixteen months younger than his brother, graduated at the top of his class from *Kodaikanal School*, at a remote hill station in western Tamil Nadu. We left India right after that, while Brad embarked on a six-month odyssey, mostly overland, following only a vague itinerary. He reached *Washington* in time to join us for Christmas, which turned out to be the final Christmas of his life.

Now, in 1984, one of my goals is to revisit *Kodaikanal*, which was such a vital part of our sons' lives. It is a peaceful secluded retreat, but first I must navigate the noise and bedlam of *Bombay* and *Madras*. Much as I long to return to India when I've been away for awhile, my first reaction upon arrival is always that of horror. What was it, I say to myself, that I was yearning for? What, amid all the cacophony and assault to the senses, could I have possibly wanted to re-experience? Who needs this total bedlam anyway? But magically it happens again. After only twenty-four hours I cease to be offended by all the smells and gaudy sights, and happily drink in the vitality surrounding me.

It helps, of course, that I still have friends in *Madras*, not in the transient foreign community so much as among full-time Madrasis. I'm greeted at the airport by my first hostess who garlands me with a fragrant sandalwood lei in welcome. I'll be hosted in two other households before I leave, three weeks hence.

The city has grown and changed since I was last here. I observe the modern shopping centers and cafes and hotels, which seem to make *Madras* more like every other city, if you ask me. The traffic, ever chaotic, has deteriorated even further. Bicycles must be proliferating like rabbits. There are still oxcarts and meandering cows and an occasional temple elephant to reflect the pace of an earlier age. Among the old-fashioned lumbering "Ambassador" cars is the unexpected flash of a jazzy new low-slung sports car, the Indian-produced "Maruti." Buses are as decrepit and overcrowded as ever. Three-wheeled rickshaws, either pedaled or motorized, complicate the equation.

The blatant cacophony of taxi horns and bicycle bells, the din of vendors peddling their wares, the disorder—by Western standards—of the traffic, how could all this have ever seemed familiar and comfortable to me? I shudder to remember that I used to drive our car here instead of using a chauffeur. Not only sounds but smells assail the senses: incense, dung burning, exotic cooking spices, fragrant flowering trees. I tune up all my sensory antenna so as not to miss a single thing.

This being January, wedding season is in full swing. Many a block you drive by at any hour of day or night has at least one brightly festooned home or wedding hall with lengthy ceremonies about to begin or already underway. My hosts take me with them to an extravagant society wedding where I'm pleased to see various familiar faces. Although I wear my dressiest outfit, it's nothing compared to the Indian women in their dazzlingly brilliant *Kancheepuram* or *Benares* silk saris, a feast for the eyes. Fortunately, one isn't expected to stay throughout the many hours that a traditional Brahmin wedding takes.

Temples abound in India, both large and colorful in public places, and small and serene in private entryways. You commonly see laughing families visiting shore temples for a fine outing as well as devout worshippers prostrating themselves before huge statues deep within temple compounds. Religion is a constant and natural part of Indian life. Now, however, the scarlet *tika* mark on a Hindu wife's forehead rarely comes from the little pot of natural *kum-kum* paste, but more often from stick-on dots like tiny band-aids purchased at the corner store. And the lacy *kolam* design on the ground just outside the front door of each home is applied with chalk rather than with the traditional rice flour.

The familiar details of life in South India come flooding back. Shun the tap water. There's always a flask of cold, filtered drinking water handy in your bathroom. Go easy at first with the well-spiced food. Enjoy the papaya, untold varieties of small bananas, tasty crispy snack foods. I love the constant lazy whir of the ceiling fan, which during the night helps disperse both the acrid fragrance of the burning "punk" coil as well as the mosquitoes. Be sure to have your own supply of toilet paper in your pocket in case you need to use a public WC. Nowadays Western toilets are quite common, but you still may find yourself, especially in rural areas, visiting a cubicle with stone footprints on each side of a shaped hole in the floor.

It's good to unwind in a friend's welcoming home, where the peace and quiet is sudden. High protective walls muffle the street noises. Shedding shoes to walk on cool terrazzo floors, sipping a tall fresh limeade or a tiny filtered South Indian coffee (rather like a foaming cappuccino), chatting with gentle warm friends of yore, these are the other side of my coin of memory. Where more than in South India could I be taken so graciously and sincerely into people's hearts and homes?

One of the first things I always do when I return here is visit my old yoga teacher and pay my respects. It was a lucky day, shortly after first arriving in *Madras*, when I was directed to yoga *acharya*, TKV Krishnamacharya, whom I called "The Professor." He was in his 80s then, still vigorous and rather intimidating. I first approached yoga with no burning desire, just simple curiosity. But having private lessons twice a week with this awe-inspiring master soon converted me in spite of myself. Not only did I learn the basic poses, or *asanas*. I also learned to breathe in a new way and to use my breath as a tool to enhance my life and steady my emotions.

Now the Professor is in his mid-90s, the marks of age minimal except that he seems much mellower, even smiling occasionally. I studied with him or with his son, Sri TKV Desikachar—equally inspiring but not at all intimidating—during my entire stay in India and I am convinced that yoga fortified me for the painful shocks soon to occur. Daily yoga practice remains an intrinsic part of my life and I have even taught yoga privately or to small classes.

My friend Radha joins me on this pilgrimage to *Kodaikanal*. We take the night train from *Madras*, and then board a local bus which navigates a serpentine two-lane road up to the hill station of *Kodaikanal*. In a country that includes the high Himalayas, other lesser mountains are considered to be only hills, even if they're seven thousand feet high, as here. The heady aroma of eucalyptus in the clear mountain air brings a flood of nostalgia.

Despite warnings that *Kodai* has changed so much, I find the growth minimal and not yet too disruptive. No fans are needed here, only fireplace fires of pungent eucy logs in the evening. My breath grows short and my legs protest at all the up and down walking necessary to get around the school campus and the star-shaped lake in the middle of this thriving little town. Radha, a romantic, declares that she would be happy to spend the rest of her life here. I'm not too sure of that, but three days is certainly inadequate, a tantalizing taste.

Radha was one of the first people I met in *Madras* who was not part of the official foreign community. In fact I rarely think of her as being an expatriate even though she originally came from northern England. Long married to an engineer from Kerala whom she met when he was training abroad, she converted to Hinduism and changed her name to Radha upon moving to India. Always dressed in *sari* or in the tunic and baggy pants outfit called *salwar-kameez*, she seemed more Indian than some of the Indian women I met, and her authentic cooking certainly rivaled any native cook's. Now, Radha welcomes this short cool trip with me; Madras's blistering heat is one thing she has never enjoyed.

I have a special reason to revisit *Kodai* this time, more than simple nostalgia. As I walk around the crowded campus of Kodaikanal International School, I see Bruce and Brad there in my mind's eye. And who is to say that Brad is not here in spirit? Less than one year after his long journey home from India to *Washington DC*, while on a weekend canoeing trip with a friend, he lost his life by drowning. Rains had swollen the Potomac River; their canoe hit a submerged boulder and capsized. Brad was nineteen years old, gentle and introspective. When Ned and I regained a modicum of balance after the profound shock of this tragedy, we had to feel grateful that our young son had experienced more in his limited years than many people do in a far longer lifetime. He loved life, he lived fully.

As a memorial, we suggested the creation of a meditation garden on the grounds of *Kodai School* where Brad had been so happy. It has taken several years to come to fruition, but on my final morning here, Brad's Garden will be formally dedicated.

After a night of constant rain the fog is heavy, fitting my mood, when I visit the lovely serene space in the early morning. I'm wearing blue jeans and maroon turtleneck, but Radha honors the occasion by donning an ivory silk sari. Her own children, somewhat younger, had admired our Brad, as did she. I'm grateful to have her with me at this time, especially as Ned could not be here.

The sun tentatively emerges by mid-morning when we gather together. It is a solemn, intimate, yet informal occasion in which several of Brad's teachers speak warmly of him. One of his classmates named Tim, now a teacher here, reads a poem he had liked, and I place a brass plaque on a huge eucalyptus tree base. I am moved by this simple ceremony, so appropriate for our modest, self-effacing son, and by the private memories which various staff members share with me. Brad's ashes are buried on a Virginia hillside, but India is home to his spirit.

Little could I have imagined then that I would return to *Kodai* with a fresh wound in my heart four years later. Bruce, our older son, had had difficulties adjusting to American life after living overseas much of his life. At age twenty-one he married another *Kodai* graduate, Vicki Gray, but it was a short-lived relationship. Dropping out of college, he took up a vagabond life, making friends easily wherever he landed, taking off for new fields whenever the mood moved: *Texas, Denver, San Francisco, Minneapolis.* When he was thirty, his restlessness finally led him to his final journey, a conscious long-deliberated choice. We could only hope that he found peace in death. On his last visit to us, he signed our guest book, "Bruce, your son from the Universe."

Despite his often stormy years at *Kodai School*, Bruce loved that high place, the hiking, the beauty of nature. When I returned there next, I was shown various trees and shrubbery that had been planted in his memory, and once again I heard tales from faculty who remembered his fun-loving vibrant presence, notable at that often staid school. I always imagine his spirit floating free in the Universe, just as he wrote.

Is it any wonder that India holds such a special place in my heart?

JAPAN Castle roof

CHAPTER 2

1986
THE TRIP OF A LIFETIME

"Hey Dorothy, let's go back to Japan together." This was my older sister Jean talking. Fifty-three years had passed since our missionary family had left *Shizuoka*, a city at the foothills of Mt. Fuji, and she yearned to revisit the place of our birth. Our parents had gone to Japan intending to spend their whole lives there. They were dismayed when they had to return home after only eleven years because the Great Depression had dried up mission funds. Although I had passed through *Tokyo* briefly several times over the years, I was sure it would be disappointing to return and see the great changes in the Japan we had known and loved.

I squashed her suggestion then, but the seed began to take root. Now, two and a half years later, after plenty of international correspondence, Jean and I find ourselves on a Canadian Pacific flight out of *Toronto* bound for *Tokyo*. It is October 3, 1986, the beginning of a four week adventure.

We're hoping to experience Japanese life and culture as intimately as possible, but we also have an eye to economy. During our lengthy planning period, the exchange rate has dropped continually so that we only get about 150 yen per US dollar. Even so, we frugal New Englanders have steeled ourselves to spend far more than proves necessary. Our carefully selected hotels cost us from US$18.70 to $32 apiece. By eating simple Japanese food at family restaurants discovered while exploring residential neighborhoods, we rarely spend more than ten dollars for lunch or breakfast—for *both* of us. A few dinners cost as much as that apiece. Some difference from the five dollar cups of coffee we have been warned to expect.

An elderly Japanese doctor who had maintained contact with our mother during all those years, has been our initial means of making connections. Gradually, through Dr. Sekiguchi, our travel arrangements have taken on the dimensions of a state visit. Our mother has followed all of our plans with envy and amazement, thrilled that we are going to revisit scenes from the happiest decade of her life. Just two weeks before we leave for Japan, she dies peacefully in her sleep at age ninety-two. I'm sure her spirit will accompany us on our travels.

After the long flight it is great to be personally welcomed at Narita airport by a friend of Dr. S's. En route to our modest *Tokyo* hotel near Ueno Park, we eagerly ogle the modern buildings, the laundry hanging out on balconies, and the occasional older woman wearing a kimono. After resting up a bit, we go to call on Dr. Sekiguchi at his lovely unpretentious traditional home. He is eighty years old and still practicing medicine part-time. His tiny gray wife serves us tea and tangerines as we haltingly try to reconnect. Although we can hardly remember, he loves telling us about his student days when he roomed with our family and studied English. By now his English is pretty rusty, but his daughter and granddaughter arrive after a bit and ease the conversation. We all end up going to a nearby restaurant for an elegant dinner, seated at a low table on the woven tatami floor, Japanese style.

Two days later we take the train to another *Tokyo* suburb to spend the night with a second Japanese family. The lady of the house, Takiko, was my best friend when I was a tiny tot in *Shizuoka*, although I don't remember her. A bundle of energy, petite Takiko, with the help of gawky Shigeo, her English-speaking collegian son, have been writing to me and have arranged an array of activities for our pleasure. Takiko stops to buy homemade tofu from a street vendor en route from the station to her home — one of the ingredients in our delicious family style dinner.

Early the next morning, Takiko, her husband Hiroichi, and Shigeo pile us into their diesel Isuzu, where Jean and I both feel very large and embarrassed by the extent of our luggage. The drive of nine hours includes several sightseeing stops before we reach the city of our birth, *Shizuoka*. Nothing looks vaguely familiar, although we wander around that evening hoping to see something that reminds us of our childhood.

The following day we all go for a brief climb on the slopes of Mt. Fuji. Only in July and August is the top of the mountain open to climbers. Now October, it even snowed the day before. Beyond the inevitable clouds, the peak appears to be right above us. We trudge up a short way through slippery lava gravel on Mt. Hoei, a spur at the side of Fujiyama, which has three volcanic craters of its own. Just for this occasion we have brought along hiking shoes and parkas, thick socks and caps, which prove to be quite unnecessary. Pretty funny, Japanese climbers are dressed in everything from traditional kimono to high heels and tight skirts. By the time we make our way down through a peaceful grove to the parking lot and restaurant, fog has rolled in, completely obliterating any further glimpse of the symmetrical peak.

During our five days in the *Shizuoka* area, we visit the site of "our" mission church — now a shop selling sewing machines — and of "our" house — now an Episcopal church, which is having a bazaar the next day, just like at home. We stay for two nights each with two different Japanese families. The hostess in each home had been a kindergarten classmate of mine. One of the functions of our mission had been running the very successful Dojin kindergarten, with my mother as principal. In fact, one day we meet at a Buddhist temple in nearby *Shimizu* for a kindergarten reunion lunch. Among the five Japanese people there, little English is spoken and our Japanese is minimal, but somehow we manage to cross the barriers of language. For one thing, at my clever sister's suggestion, we have brought with us small pocket photo albums showing our families and lives. Also, we share a collection of colorful postcards from both Florida and Vermont, Jean's home. We may have forgotten the language but certainly have not forgotten how to use chopsticks.

Gift-giving is a big part of the social scene in Japan. We have spent considerable thought in planning what to take to the many people who will be hosting us. Well, the postcards are a hit as icebreakers and to give to casual acquaintances as small mementoes. For special friends we have larger items. Jean's boxes of little maple sugar cakes from Vermont are popular. Somehow we neglected to anticipate that we would be getting gifts in return. They are seldom designed for world travelers with limited baggage. Between the gifts we receive and our many purchases along the way, we each have to pack and send home a couple of full boxes before leaving the country. We're happy to find that post offices sell several sizes of carton, with all necessary tape and strapping. No problem. When they arrive many weeks later, these boxes evoke all the memories of the trip again.

One unexpected gift never makes it to the post office. To get Japanese yen at a bank requires much patience and paperwork, so we learn to exchange several US travelers' checks at a time. One afternoon when I cash in three such checks, it turns out that a fourth check has mysteriously torn out without my noticing. Several hours later, after the banks have closed, we receive a surprise visit at our secluded ryokan—Japanese-style inn—from the pretty little bank teller, bowing and blushing and apologizing profusely for the mistake—mine, not hers, of course. After returning my orphaned check, she formally presents us with a beautifully wrapped box of leaf-shaped confections. We can hardly make it back to our room before bursting into laughter at the wonder of it all. Where but in Japan would one be presented with a fancy gift while having one's error corrected by the bank?

Before leaving *Shizuoka*, we even have the chance to do a little farming—digging sweet potatoes in a backyard garden—which makes Jean feel at home. One Japanese friend, upon hearing of Jean's fifty-acre Vermont farm, opines that in overcrowded Japan that would be declared a national park. As for me, imagine my surprise to find one of our dinner hostesses is a fellow basket maker, who proceeds to teach us how to weave split bamboo bracelets and tiny finger rings. I still have mine.

When we first heard we would spend two nights each at two different homes in *Shizuoka*, we had dreaded the frequent packing up. But it turns out that we have so much fun getting to know these people, trying to surmount the language barrier, laughing a lot and experiencing real Japanese home life, that we wouldn't have wanted it otherwise. Japanese people are gracious and unfailingly courteous, but their hospitality is formal by our standards. They entertain you at a restaurant for dinner, rarely at home.

We feel very privileged to be welcomed as overnight guests in several households, all Japanese style homes. It reflects the warm appreciation for our parents' influence on these families so many years ago. It also breaks us in to sleeping on the springy tatami floor under fat quilted comforters that appear out of a cupboard when night falls. I believe that we slept in a Western bed only two nights during this whole month. But not all Japanese homes have the serene uncluttered spaces that we had expected. Modern influences are evident in the crocheted tissue box covers, antimacassars and fussy decorations that adorn at least some of the homes we visit. They're probably proud of how Western they are.

Two or more hours on the Shinkanzen (Bullet Train) takes us from *Shizuoka* to *Kyoto*, past rice fields and ever-changing views of Mount Fuji. *Kyoto* is wonderful, for a first-timer or an old Japan hand. Part of its charm for us comes from the two small ryokans where we stay; one has only four rooms, the other nine. You leave your shoes at the front entrance and slide into slippers which you in turn leave outside the sliding door of your room. To walk down the polished wooden hallway to the toilet or bath, you again need slippers. Many times we find the toilet seats are electrically heated, a wonderful touch in a cold room. Soaking in the deep steamy ofuro—bath—is the perfect ending for a tired tourist's day. Our baths and showers here may get us clean, but they can't begin to loosen the kinks and soothe the soul as a proper ofuro can. Back in the bedroom, you may have trouble crawling around the matted tatami floor on your knees, but rosy and warm from the bath, you nestle cozily into the puffy futon—comforter—on that spongy woven floor and sleep peacefully.

We get around *Kyoto* by public bus and train, except for one full day when we take a commercial tour to the temple town of *Nara*. Seeing those sights with a professional guide that day is enlightening, but it sure does seem strange to be among Westerners only, and to eat a mediocre Western meal at the Nara Hotel after our steady diet of Japanese food for the previous ten days. Our Japanese tour guide croons pop songs to his passengers as the bus takes us back to the hotel.

One day we make our way by train to another temple town on the outskirts of *Kyoto* to observe the annual *Ningyo Kuyo* or doll requiem. Favorite worn-out dolls are taken to this temple to be dedicated before being cremated. We have read that "the people pray wholeheartedly in order to thank and console the dolls which have been entertaining and comforting them for a long time." A very solemn atmosphere prevails. It seems a mighty strange custom to us, but perhaps this is more emotionally satisfying than relegating a beloved worn-out doll to the trash heap. Afterward, everyone is served a simple lunch on long low red-covered tables arranged on a broad stone deck, the gentle hills watching over us.

Another day we take a bus to *Arashiyama*, where my friend, Chizuko, a fellow yoga teacher, lives with her American husband and three small children. Some seventeen of her students meet with Chizuko and me at a hotel for a wide-ranging discussion of yoga in our lives. The *Kyoto* newspaper interviews us, which may give her some good publicity. Back at their home, Jean loves playing with the children, who are about the ages of her own two grandsons. But Jean's grandsons are better behaved than six-year-old Yuma, who runs around wildly, defying our stereotype of well-mannered Asian children. We are told that until a certain unspecified age anything goes; after that, obedience is required.

Finally it is time to reverse directions. It takes us most of one day going by rail to *Sendai*, which is almost as far north of *Tokyo* as *Kyoto* is south. We love traveling on Japanese trains, which are very clean and efficient. This is not the first time that we find ourselves the object of discreet curiosity, the only foreigners in a very Japanese environment. A teenager named Fumiko comes to sit with us and practice her English. Other women offer us samples of their snack foods and we return the favor. They are amused that one of our bags of candy contains small melt-in-your-mouth sweets that are meant for toddlers. We have to change trains twice; the final segment is one-and-a-half hours on a local, late in the evening. Many formally dressed but slightly tipsy men get on and off that last train, obviously coming home from weddings or parties.

We have been asked more than once why we are going to *Sendai*, as it is definitely off the tourist beat. It is in a beautiful part of Japan, especially near by Matsushima Bay, and there are many historic temples and mountain sites. But our interest is more personal. In 1923 our parents had designed a summer house and had it built at a seaside colony for foreigners some distance from *Sendai*. In that rustic wooded cottage we had enjoyed blissful summers for all of our early years. Although *Sendai* itself was almost leveled during World War II, we have reason to believe that our beloved *Takayama* might have survived, though in what condition we don't know.

It is a day for exploration. We take a local train, then an almost empty country bus. It feels like the middle of nowhere when we get off at a beach, quite deserted except for a solo young surfboarder. Now late October, the day is windy and raw. There is nobody around to ask, but after a couple of false tries, we trudge toward two low hills which flank a curving beach. It begins to look familiar but somehow smaller than in our memory. Yes, this is indeed the *Takayama* protected development that we knew more than half a century before. An identifying sign reassures us.

After scrambling over a padlocked gate, we wander around the pine-wooded hillsides, starting to recognize familiar landmarks, and finally — wonder of wonders — find our own beloved house. No question about it. Except for the inevitable weathering which has darkened the natural wood, and a few minor alterations, including a TV antenna, it looks just as we remember it.

When I get back to Florida, I compare new and old snapshots; the changes in those fifty-three years are truly minimal. Finding that remembered cottage, scene of our most idyllic childhood memories, is without doubt the real "high" in a month filled with highs. We sit on the front steps munching snacks, laughing and crying, wishing we could share this nostalgic moment with our other sister. As the eldest, Ruth has the sharpest memories of Japan, but is physically unable to travel here with us.

Back in *Tokyo* for our final few days, we stay at our original ryokan, with its formal garden and small musical stream. The desk clerk there likes to ask us if we are futagi—twins, a new word for us. I suppose Westerners all look alike to most Asian observers, or maybe Jean and I look more alike the older we get. Our last excursion is to *Nikko* to view that famous temple. We have seen very few kimonos being worn anywhere except at the occasional hotel wedding. But here there is an enchanting family group of three generations, with all but the infant dressed in elegant traditional attire.

October is popular for school field trips. No shrine or park or scenic wonder do we visit throughout Japan without seeing obedient groups of uniformed school children of every age. Within the older groups there is always a child slightly bolder than the rest who will, upon seeing us, immediately say, "Haro Haro." We always reply, but they rarely know the next lesson, how to respond to "What is your name?" or "How old are you?"

It is quite a surprise to us that we can get around so well with our minimal Japanese language. Most of our childhood language skills have long since vanished. People are always eager to help us. Once we are rescued in Ueno Station by a trio of tall lanky students—basketball players maybe—who rightly guess that we are not sure where to catch our train. They shepherd us to the right gate. At one of our *Shizuoka* home stays, our hostess is a jovial artist named Reiko— sounds like Leiko to us. Her next-door neighbor, a sharp young English teacher, drops by regularly to translate and make sure we have everything we need. He probably welcomes the opportunity to practice his English with native speakers.

Likewise, ordering at a restaurant proves amazingly simple. Either the aroma from a soba stall lures us in for a bowl of buckwheat noodle soup, or more often the restaurant window display solves the problem. We can simply point to the very realistic wax model of the particular dish we like the looks of, with its price displayed below, and the waiter will bring it to our table. Of course, it helps that we are familiar with a range of Japanese cuisine and can usually recognize the ingredients from the display. We also discover that the basement level of large department stores is where the food is. We often skip a proper meal after having grazed past many counters offering free samples of their specialties. Even an unbalanced sampling of sembei rice crackers, pickles, and tiny buttery cookies satisfies the taste buds and ignites a sense of nostalgia.

We return to Takiko's house for our final night in Japan and her family drive us the next day to Narita airport. After the inevitable sequence of formal posed snapshots of all of us, Jean and I drag our expanded baggage through security and onto Canadian Pacific once again. We depart at seven pm; we arrive in *Toronto* at 7:45 pm the same day. Ah, the miracle of modern flight—and the International Date Line.

Isn't it appropriate that our *Toronto* hotel at the start and end of this incredible trip is named Valhalla? I seem to remember from grade school mythology that Valhalla was the castle hall of the Norse gods. We pinch ourselves in wonder that each day of the journey has been filled with such sheer delight. We have met long-forgotten friends and made new ones, tasted half-remembered flavors, and reveled in the familiar smells and sounds of that magical land of our birth.

An unexpected joy is learning new things about my own sister. Jean and I have never spent much time together as adults, so it is a surprise to find that the very same details catch our eyes as we explore new surroundings. Our antenna are out and active. I tend to study the map and go forging ahead toward a destination while Jean patiently follows, saying "rots of ruck." I laugh until I cry more than once. We giggle like kids—which we often feel like again—at some of our language gaffes and misunderstandings. It has been a voyage of discovery on more than one level.

Only traveling with my compatible sister could I have experienced such a thrilling memory trip. Thanks, Jean. This wouldn't have been the trip of a lifetime without you.

THAILAND After the river bath

CHAPTER 3

1990–1992
YOU COULD JOIN THE PEACE CORPS

Who said that? Where did that come from? I wake up one morning with the message floating in my head, "You could join the Peace Corps."

Now I have plenty else on my mind right then, taking care of a terminally ill husband. I am too absorbed in sharing these last few weeks and days with him to worry about my future. But the inevitable happens, and Ned dies of esophageal cancer, too young, in July 1989. Amidst all the necessary paperwork and lawyer's appointments and decision-making that ensues, that little phrase keeps coming back to haunt me. I was not ready to give up our ever-changing overseas life when Ned retired from the US Foreign Service in 1979, but then we settled into a wonderfully amiable *Sarasota* life. Now here it is ten years later, and I, at sixty-two, feel I am still young enough to live overseas again, if only I can find the right situation. Far horizons beckon.

During the next year I scout out every possible international placement, not only the Peace Corps. Without formal career experience whereby to sell myself, I compile a resume listing all those skills I had mastered as the wife of a diplomat abroad. I call upon all my friends still involved in the international scene for ideas. One job that momentarily catches my fancy is as the administrator of a refugee camp in Pakistan. Never mind that Pakistan was far from our favorite posting thirty years earlier, nor do I have the requisite managerial experience for such a big job. In hindsight, I'm grateful that they weren't hard up enough to accept my application.

On my Peace Corps form I designate a preference for any country in Asia. But when the recruiter calls me, Central America is the only option. And they want me to teach farming practices—I who have a brown thumb. I'm sure my farmer students there would end up teaching me instead. Obviously their needs don't coincide with my interests and skills. So much for the Peace Corps. Anyway, I'm really keen to return to Asia, even if I have to pay for the privilege of volunteering. I was born in Japan and spent twenty-odd adult years in different Asian countries stretching in an arc from Taiwan westward to Pakistan. When friends imagine us to be disappointed at never having had a European assignment, I assure them that our hearts were firmly entrenched in Southeast and South Asia. Those Foreign Service years, not all of them easy, were still a glorious experience for the Conlon family.

Now it is September 1990 and I hold in my hand a round trip ticket to *Bangkok*. I've packed things up, held a yard sale, and put lots of beloved possessions in storage. Who knows how I'll feel about living in this house one year or more from now? To sell it seems too big a decision at this point, so I'm renting it out. I am putting my Florida life on hold for at least a year to live in Thailand as a volunteer with WorldTeach, a branch of the Harvard Institute for International Development. I board the plane with only one large bag and a carry-on, wondering if I've thought of everything I'll need for the year or more ahead. The adventure begins.

When twenty-six eager volunteers arrive in *Bangkok*, it's immediately obvious that I am the only senior. In fact Phil, a returned Peace Corps volunteer and the next eldest in this young crowd, is less than half my age. Many of them are fresh out of college, from all over the USA and Canada, about equal numbers of men and women. Our first month is spent on orientation, to introduce us to the intricacies of the Thai language, give us an overview of Thai history and culture, and—most importantly—provide some basic teaching tools and practice for our upcoming classroom placements.

This month also breaks us in to *Bangkok* heat. We're told how lucky we are to be starting our year in October, considered a cool month by the Thais. But even this Floridian finds it mighty hot. Floor and ceiling fans are totally inadequate. One of my first purchases is a length of printed cotton called a *pasin*, worn as a wrapped skirt by Thai women. Think *sarong*. A similar plaid garment, called a *pakama*, is worn by men. Mine adapts nicely as a sleeping garment, cooler than a sheet. We learn to eat Thai style, sitting on the floor, and I relish the pungent new flavors—lemon grass, *galagang*, lots of ginger, hot green papaya salad.

Thai students are given English instruction from an early age, yet the English coming out of their mouths is virtually unrecognizable. The inflections of their tonal *Pasa Thai*—Thai language—are naturally applied to English words, with strange results. Their English grammar and vocabulary may be excellent; their pronunciation is impossible. That is why we native English speakers are so welcome here, whether or not we have ever taught the language. Most of us have not.

My fellow volunteers fan out to various assignments in Thai government schools around the country. Much as I dislike city living—*Bangkok* was then a city of over four million souls—I have requested *Bangkok* on the theory that my language inadequacies will be less of a problem there. I have lived in many different countries surrounded by many different languages, but my skill at anything other than English is poor. I thoroughly believe in *studying* different languages as a window into the culture and psychology of the people, but when it comes to speaking, I am hopelessly inept. Fortunately, speaking *Pasa Thai* in class is discouraged, a rule that I'm happy to observe. Eventually I absorb enough basic Thai to explore the city and to bargain in the markets, but I never conquer the subtleties of that tonal language. One useful phrase I do learn is *mai pen rai,* which means "never mind" or "cool it" or "take it easy." A perfect expression of the Thai philosophy of life.

What will my assigned school be like? *Borphitpimuk Mahamek,* which I never learn to pronounce correctly, is a vocational institution of over two thousand students aged sixteen to twenty, mostly girls. I don't have to leave my shoes outside the door, as the thirty-five or forty students in each of my classes do. Their uniforms are always crisp and clean. As the honored *ajaan*—teacher—I wear skirts and tops, never sleeveless, and closed shoes. Except for Bill, an Australian, I'm the only foreign teacher in this whole school. I immediately hit it off with *Woraphorn,* the head of the English Department, who studied in Australia. She is a young mother, dynamic and fun, who rides to work on her motorbike. My other favorite among the English teachers is *Ajaan Sakul,* nearing retirement, but still younger than I.

Thai students are attentive and eager, all except the three or four boys in each class, who often sleep at their desks when they bother to appear at all. Students in Asian schools are not expected to participate much, simply to listen and repeat back. But how can you learn a language without speaking up? Before the year is over I coax them into being interactive, as we play language games, sing, and do role playing. How they do love to sing and act out "Hokey Pokey." I dream up new Thailand oriented verses to "This Land Is Your Land" for one class to sing at an assembly program.

It's really quite fun designing activities to get my students to use English in every-day situations, at the same time following the curriculum enough that they'll be able to pass the standardized exams. One day my most advanced class creates a virtual marketplace, with the best students playing the role of vendors and the others wandering around as shoppers, haggling for items just as they would in the local market. The hard part for them is to remember to speak only English while they're doing this. During a textbook lesson on Hobbies, I'm bemused by a tally of the students' favorite "hobbies." At the top is Shopping, followed closely by Sleeping. I'm thrilled that a few list Reading until I discover that what they read is comic books. In another of my scheduled classes I work with the Thai teachers on their pronunciation and English conversation skills. Occasionally I'm asked to record tapes in the language lab. My work schedule is very full, and I find I love it.

When I leave school each day to walk through the bustling market to my nearby walk-up room, I'm bushed. My spacious room, on the third floor above a small mom-and-pop store, is pretty basic, but it does have a ceiling fan, a telephone and a tiny front balcony. Without a kitchen, I'm lucky to overlook a lane that is a veritable food court. Each morning I awake to the aroma of garlic cooking outside my window. Much as I enjoy Thai meals in *Sarasota* restaurants, eating street food all this year in *Bangkok* is quite a different experience. Restaurants? Not really, either storefronts or wheeled carts, but always producing fresh cooked, pungent, delectable dishes. When I arrive home after nineteen months away, I am surprised to have lost weight, because I had certainly feasted—even gorged—to my heart's content. My food costs me between two and three dollars a day, lucky, since my monthly salary from the Royal Thai Government is meager.

I never buy my meals in the big open market where they are pre-cooked and all too often covered with flies. But my fellow teachers get their favorite dishes there and carry them home in plastic bags to serve to their families for dinner. Although I'm fairly adventurous, I never get up the courage to try the crispy spicy grasshoppers being grilled, no matter how tempting the aroma. What are some of my favorite foods? *Pad thai* is undoubtedly the most ubiquitous national dish, but I quickly discover that it is made quite differently from one place to another. My favorite wheeled vendor serves a *pad thai* full of crunchy bean sprouts and chopped peanuts atop the noodles. Probably I watch him make it for me at least twice a week. I eat it seated on a stool on the sidewalk, or may take it back to my room to dine alone at my desk.

A refreshing treat which I indulge in a couple of times a week comes from a charming young woman who creates syrupy slurpies of vile colors in a blender. When I am too hot and tired to eat or read or even sleep, one of these coolers always revives me. And the amazing thing is that I never get sick from all that unpurified ice. Thailand has many delectable tropical fruits, but I'm pretty careful about buying cut-up chunks of papaya or pineapple which have been displayed on a cart for who knows how long. Without a frig, I can't keep fresh fruit in my room, except bananas.

One snack which I get quite addicted to is a round ball of greasy fried dough, almost the size of a tangerine, filled with a dollop of sweet bean paste. It doesn't sound so wonderful, but believe me, it hits the spot as an afternoon pick-me-up. Although there are McDonald's and other American fast food restaurants in *Bangkok*, I never go near them. Only toward the end of my stay, when a Dunkin Donuts opens up a block away, do I treat myself occasionally to some doughnut holes, just for a taste of home. Mind you, I never go near Dunkin Donuts in *Sarasota*.

Living in such a noisy bustling city accentuates the loneliness of my existence, quite unanticipated. All those years I had lived overseas previously I had been surrounded by family and a network of expatriate colleagues and friends. Here, petite *Woraphorn*, my charming department head, and the other Thai teachers I work with are unfailingly kind and friendly, but their hour or more commute to their homes by bus or motorcycle precludes any after-hours socializing. Likewise, meeting foreigners and getting together with them is not easy, given the horrendous traffic conditions. Public buses are numerous, sardine full, and maddeningly slow. Three-wheeled *tuk-tuks* or motorcycle taxis are faster but dangerous on main thoroughfares.

My school and room are in the heart of the city, far from the residential areas popular with *farang*—foreigners. One wonderful expat couple invites me to their air conditioned home for dinner occasionally, a delight despite the two-hour bus ride getting to their side of town. How to show my appreciation? From the flower vendor I often buy a few sprays of delicate orchids for only a couple of dollars. Imagine!

Easy-going Rob, one of our volunteers from California, lives in my building and frequently drops in to chat. He can't get over how beautiful the girls in his classes are. But he really suffers when the foul *Bangkok* air affects his asthma. Some of the other WorldTeachers stop by when they come to the capital city. I particularly look forward to seeing Phil, who taught for the Peace Corps in the Philippines; we have more in common.

Gradually I learn my way around this busy city, often nipping into an air conditioned shop just to get a breath of cool air during a long hot exploratory walk. My *Bangkok* map is in shreds within the first few months. When I lose my way, I look for a pharmacy because someone there will invariably be able to speak English. I discover the American Library and end up consuming books at a great rate. One happy evening, flipping the dials, I find a Thai radio station that plays classical

Western music—music to my ears. With a good book and music, being alone is no longer lonely. I don't miss TV at all, and am amazed one morning to find throngs of students and faculty watching a CNN broadcast at my school auditorium. The Gulf War has just started, a wake-up call bringing me back into the wider world.

Slowly a few other accessible activities open up. Moonlighting, I am hired to test the English skills of Vietnamese refugees about to be relocated to the US. An occasional fun assignment is in the staff training program at the posh Oriental Hotel. I take the hotel ferryboat across the Chao Phraya River and sit in a little private dining room, studying the menu. Trying to act like a demanding foreign tourist, I ask lots of stupid questions of the trainees and deliberately misunderstand them, just to test their English and their people skills. Amazing how many different regional accents I can conjure up for this exercise. For this play-acting I receive a small stipend plus an elegant Thai meal—a step up from my usual street food.

When Christmas arrives, I'm surprised at how colorfully this Buddhist city decorates for our Christian holiday. I even go to a concert of Handel's Messiah presented by an international chorus, a nostalgic experience. About that time I hear of a Sweet Adelines group which meets weekly to sing together at a downtown hotel. When I join them, it opens up my social life a little, singing with both Thai and foreign women.

Shopping in *Bangkok* can be great fun, particularly at the sprawling weekend *Chatuchak* market, but since I'm watching my pennies, I don't want to be tempted. Only when foreign friends come to town do I take them there to wander and wonder at the live animals, flowers, foodstuffs, ceramics, and other diverse merchandise for sale. It's a great place whether you buy or not, more fun than the modern upscale malls where my students hang out. Today, one of my favorite coffee mugs, with a traditional blue and white geometric design, came from *Chatuchak* and cost about one dollar. It always brings back memories.

We volunteers are provided housing—for me a simple furnished room with compact shower but no kitchen, which costs the Ministry of Education one hundred and twenty dollars per month rent. I've hung some colorful travel posters and bought a few plants for the balcony, which do not last long in this bad air. For much of the year, the only way I can get to sleep in the heat, even using the ceiling fan, is by taking a cold shower at bedtime. A nearby laundry is inexpensive but will not handle lingerie. Extreme modesty is a basic tenet of the Thai culture. That means that I must hand-wash my bras and panties and hang them up on the rooftop. I can't quite picture some of our male volunteers doing that.

We are paid at the same rate as Thai teachers—3,500 baht ($140) a month in my case. That doesn't sound like much, but it's considered a respectable salary for a Thai college graduate, and it's adequate for this frugal New Englander, given the many bargains in *Bangkok*. Only when I take trips during school holidays do I need to dip into my US bank account.

Now it's March, the start of spring semester break, and I'm on my way to India and Australia to visit friends. I hardly dare tell my Thai colleagues about these plans, they are so far from the realm of possibility for them. But I feel myself emerging out of my constrained volunteer self into my old traveler self. Nowadays, whenever I meet people who loved touring in Thailand, they envy me my long stay there. They rave about the glittering bejeweled *wats*—Buddhist temples—the wonderful shopping and the charming people. Little do they know how the country appears from underneath its smiling facade, through the eyes of a typical low-income resident.

Every country puts on its best face for visitors, of course, but actually living there opens your eyes to social ills and unappealing cultural differences. Thailand bills itself as the Land of Smiles, and indeed smiling faces abound. How often do those smiles mask major problems at home or at work? Even as modernization spreads throughout Thai cities, rural families still send their daughters to *Bangkok* or abroad to become sex workers. And the male in Thailand rules supreme, in the home and in the working world. Thailand is a country of great beauty and charm, but when you live there, some of the first gloss rubs off. It's good to take a short break away.

Although my teaching contract is for only one year, I have felt definite pressure from my school to stay on for another semester. I'm not at all interested. Holidaying in India, I research the chance of doing volunteer work there for a few months after finishing my contract in *Bangkok*. The *Sarasota* house is rented out, my ticket home is valid for another six months, why not stay overseas among old friends in *Madras*?

So it is that in October, as I'm grading the last of my students' exam papers, my two sisters arrive. We are going to tour Thailand for three weeks before I pack up and relocate. My painfully acquired Thai language, basic though it is, is adequate to escort them on this private excursion. An overnight train takes us north to delightful *Chiang Mai*, followed by a day trip from *Mai Hong Son* to *Mai Aw* in the Golden Triangle, hamlets near the Burmese border. Eventually we make our way down to *Koh Samet*, a laid-back southern island far from the typical tourist beaches.

I've had great fun designing this itinerary to give my sisters a taste of the whole country, a broader view than the stunning sights of *Bangkok*, all that most tourists see. Jean is always ready for anything. Ruth, frail from a lifetime of illnesses, surprises us with her energy and stamina. I may be the youngest, but they're willing for me to be the tour leader. We see fields of opium poppies, get up close to working elephants, and view the process of silk-making—one of

Thailand's most exquisite products. My sisters enjoy the whole adventure as much as do I, and amazingly, nothing goes wrong. It is a wonderful finale to my year of *Bangkok* living, and for them a view into an Asian culture quite different from Japan, where we three spent our early childhood.

Settling into a relaxed life in *Madras*, where the Conlon family lived for five years, is easy. I find a role for myself teaching English at an orphanage school. These fun-loving little Indian kids are enchanting. Volunteering here is quite different from Thailand, since I can make up my own curriculum. I rent a room in a modern apartment and ride a public bus or motor rickshaw everywhere. I not only study yoga with my long-time teacher but he recruits me to do some editing and interviewing for their publications. My friend Radha and others invite me home for holidays and social events. Although it's been fifteen years since we left India, *Madras* feels like home to me. No small town, it still has very little of the noise and air pollution which make *Bangkok* so trying. It gives me a comfortable and satisfying few months before my air ticket runs out and I turn homeward.

Almost nineteen months to the day after leaving *Sarasota*, I finally set foot here again. It's been a fantastic adventure, quenching my thirst for travel for at least the near future. Being so far away has given me clarity about my ongoing life here. To quote T.S. Eliot, "We shall not cease from exploration—and the end of all our exploring will be to arrive where we started and know the place for the first time."

This lovely house was perfect for Ned and me, but I no longer need it. Within the next two months I sell it and move into a secluded condo, ready to start a whole new life. *Bangkok* inner city life taught me that I need to live close to nature. Now, I can almost imagine monkeys swinging from the jungly vegetation surrounding my second story home. Cardinals, woodpeckers and even an owl are regular visitors to my woods. Also, living sparingly in my *Bangkok* walk-up, I learned how much unnecessary stuff we allow to clutter up our lives. I don't wish to live such a Spartan life again, but it is satisfying to pare down to my most cherished possessions. The fewer items vying for my attention, the more precious they become.

I'm not sorry to have had the WorldTeach experience; it taught me a lot about myself. Being away alone for so long was a real challenge and made me treasure my friends here. Once settled back into a simple lifestyle, I dream up a way to feed my wandering spirit with less stress. Since Florida winters are a marketable item, I decide to rent out my condo for two or three months each year, which will help pay for extended travel. Wherever in the world I go, I'll try to include a volunteering stint to give me an inside perspective while doing something useful. And when I return from new adventures each spring, my leafy *Sarasota* hideaway will be here to welcome me home.

TANZANIA Pounding maize

CHAPTER 4

1994
POMMERN BRICK BRIGADE

Four weeks after leaving the comforts of *Sarasota*, I arrive in the East African country of Tanzania, which is to be the core experience in my 1994 wanderings. On this, my maiden visit to East Africa, I start with a short classy safari on the Masai Mara of Kenya, then travel by bus to *Arusha*, just over the border into Tanzania. Eventually I make it here to the capital city of *Dar-es Salaam*, which means "Haven of Peace."

Located right on the Indian Ocean, *Dar* reminds me somewhat of my beloved *Madras* in India, where I lived for five years and have just revisited. Both have a decidedly seedy sort of charm and beautiful flamboyant trees. The humid heat is likewise familiar. My optometrist would be proud of me for wearing dark glasses constantly in Africa, a habit I have yet to cultivate in Florida. Walking on the streets, one is constantly greeted with big smiles and the greeting, *Jambo Mama*. I keep a firm grip on my waist pack even as I return the greeting and smile.

In *Nairobi* I was warned to be very wary when walking downtown, and *never* to go out alone at night. Although I feel no sense of danger, it seems prudent to follow the same advice in this Tanzanian city. Matter of fact, during my first day of exploring *Dar-es Salaam*, I have a questionable episode. I have learned to walk briskly, with purpose, as though I know where I'm going in strange cities even when I don't. In this downtown area there are plenty of men lounging in doorways, unemployed and observant.

I suddenly hear an African voice speaking to me and realize that a tall, handsome young man is dogging my footsteps. He tells me how dangerous it is for me to walk alone and that he, an off-duty policeman, will be happy to accompany and protect me. Without even turning to acknowledge that I hear him, I march right along, keeping an eye on his reflection in the empty store windows beside me. And of course keeping close hold on my fanny pack. After several more attempts to offer his services, he gives up and I get back to my hotel without incident. Is this indeed a friendly offer? Am I being too suspicious?

I have some trouble finding a cheap clean hotel in *Dar*, because the Y, which I had planned on using, has no private rooms. But the Mawenzi—thirty-five dollars with A/C—works fine for a few days before I switch to the upscale Agip Motel to join the Global Volunteers group I'll be working with for the next couple of weeks. Since most of our contingent is not arriving till Saturday, I hop the hydrofoil over to the fabled spice island of *Zanzibar* to explore for a couple of days.

Although *Zanzibar*, so romantic sounding, has been a part of Tanzania since 1964, we have to go through Immigration upon landing. And it feels like a different country, with strong Arab influence. The architecture in the city is distinctive with heavy carved doors, and the pace is even slower than in *Dar-es-Salaam*. The museum looks like a mosque; maybe it was built for that originally. The sound of the *muezzin* calling the faithful to prayer five times daily is loud and clear in my third floor hotel room.

At a private plantation out in the country, I see various fruits and spices growing: plantains, carambola — sometimes called star fruit — clove, cinnamon, pepper vines winding around poles, and more. I look in vain for ginger plants because that is one of my favorite seasonings. Farmhouses are built of mud and coral on a framework of mangrove poles. *Zanzibar* feels even hotter than the mainland, if possible. It has beautiful beaches, but I don't wander there. That turns out to be a prudent decision, as I later discover.

After this relaxing laid-back diversion, back in *Dar* I join the eight other volunteers, aged twenty-four to sixty-eight, for an introductory lunch, and meet preppy young team leader Steve. His African experience is as non-existent as mine or most of the others. Tomorrow we'll head out of town to the village of *Pommern* in the southern highlands, where we will work at a Lutheran boarding school, doing *what* is not yet clear.

I leave our orientation lunch early to join a young African whom I had chatted with on my *Arusha* bus trip. Back at his house I meet his wife, Mercy, and have a native meal. It just happens that she grew up in *Pommern*, living with an uncle and going to the very school where we will be working. When I find out how tiny and remote *Pommern* is, I realize what a coincidence this meeting is, and I am grateful for this personal contact. I also appreciate an introduction to typical African food although it seems tasteless to me after living on Indian flavors most recently.

Promptly the following morning we load gear and people into a rented van for the long ride to *Iringa*, our overnight destination in the highlands. Although the highway is much better than I had expected, it still takes us ten hours with virtually no stops to cover the three hundred miles. We drive southwest, straight through Mikumi National Park, seeing zebra, giraffe and warthogs on either side of the road. In retrospect, I know what an easy day's ride this was, but at the time we are all exhausted when we reach the Lutheran Center, a hostelry that turns out to have truly "basic" accommodations. We sleep four to a room under mosquito nets. My net is mighty holey. It is hot. Sleep is elusive.

We are only scheduled to spend one day in *Iringa*, which reminds me of *Kodaikanal*, the south Indian hill station I know so well. Meeting Lutheran Bishop Mdegella is high on our agenda, but he is unable to honor our appointment. His is the sponsoring organization for the Global Volunteers projects in Tanzania. This is Africa, with its own sense of time, we keep reminding ourselves. Phoebe Msigomba, an official at the diocese office, takes the women of our group to the bazaar that afternoon to buy *kangas*—the lengths of bright printed cotton cloth that local women drape around themselves, usually over their Western clothing. I get totally drenched to the skin twice during this frustrating day. Sudden short cloudbursts are typical. Only we Westerners seem to mind them. At least there is hot water for a recuperative shower back at the hostel. The day ends on a high note, though, with a big dinner at the home of Phoebe and husband John, with assorted other family members present. Africans are so warm and hospitable.

Now it is Tuesday and even though there is no truck in sight to take us to *Pommern*, the sun is shining. Our spirits lift. Sure enough, by mid-day we move into high gear at the promise of a repaired truck. We descend upon the market to purchase vast quantities of rice, beans, kerosene, cooking oil, sleeping mats, plastic buckets. It all seems quite haphazard to me, but at last we and our gear are stuffed onto the big flatbed Lutheran truck and driving out of *Iringa* by two p.m. The mats barely help to cushion us during this very rough ride; we jolt along an incredibly bad road for three long hours. We have to get out and push more than once. And we have covered just thirty miles. But our spirits are high to be arriving at last in

Pommern — sometimes kiddingly called Pommerini — and we're eager to get busy with whatever work we may be assigned.

The German mission bungalow, a solid brick building with large rooms, is where we'll be housed. With virtually no furniture, only the sleeping mats and our sleeping bags protect us from the hard floors. Most of us suspend mosquito nets overhead. The two men have a smaller room in a different wing. Four of our women are on the ground floor; I am upstairs with three others. Some Tanzanian teachers live in smaller side rooms. We are carefully shown the WC pit hidden in thick grass away from the house, with instructions to call out *hodi hodi* as we approach, in case someone is already there. The filthy inside bathroom is in such a state of disrepair that we're unable to use it. Neither here nor in the kitchen are there any drain pipes, so our new buckets get put to prompt and heavy use.

Without electricity, our meals are cooked for us on kerosene and charcoal stoves by cheerful, plump Violet. She is the young school librarian, but thanks to her excellent English, she's been assigned to help us. We also help her, on a rotating schedule. Learning how to cook basic simple African dishes is not a bad experience, but cleaning up under these conditions isn't much fun. A lot of oil is used in the food, and with limited hot water and inadequate lighting, it's almost impossible to get dishes as clean as we would like. Thievery is so pervasive — an accepted part of African culture — that no supplies or utensils can be left outside the locked storeroom. Cooking with scarcely a proper pot or implement in a dark damp little kitchen bothers us far more than it does Violet.

Global Volunteers espouses the concept of "service learning" and I quite agree in principle. We're here to do whatever needs to be done. Some of us with teaching experience had rather expected to be tapped to teach, but no, we're needed to work on assorted construction projects. Lo and Susan volunteer for the carpentry shop, to plane and hammer chairs for the classrooms. Peggy and Marta, Nancy and Deana, joke about how quickly a new dorm will rise out of the grassy field from their heavy digging efforts. Steve, the coordinator, leads nightly team-building group sessions which quickly deteriorate into gripe sessions. An aspiring lawyer, he's young and lacks skill at group dynamics. He stays apart from our daily activities except on the final day when he comes around with camera to take "official photographs," presumably for Global Volunteers headquarters back in Minnesota.

Will and Lois and I choose to work on a small brick staff house which has been started by previous volunteers. It proves to be a more satisfying activity than the others, though the visible results of our nine days of work are minimal. In every case, students are supposed to work alongside us. Hand-made bricks have been drying in a big pile out in a field, and it is our job to get them to the house where the mason will mortar them in place. Rather than trudge back and forth from the field with an armload, we organize a line of workers and pass the bricks from one to another, as in an old-fashioned bucket brigade.

Our days start early with only tea or coffee available before we are supposed to start work at seven-thirty. Then it's back to the dorm for a breakfast of hot cornmeal porridge at ten. That is the African meal pattern, but we don't work well without breakfast first, so are delighted to find women vending *mandazis*, a sort of fried dough ball, just down our lane. They're heavy and tasteless but we love them. After a break for mid-morning breakfast we go back to work till one o'clock lunchtime. Some of us work again for an hour in the afternoon, but it's free time for all after three-thirty. This is the time of day that young neighborhood kids like to come play in our big front yard, gradually getting closer and closer to where we're sitting on the broad veranda, till one or more of us bounces down to play ball with them. Dinner, which is a mirror image of lunch, is supposed to appear by seven-thirty and occasionally does.

Violet quickly discovers that the African staple dish, called *ugali* in Tanzania, *sadza* in Zimbabwe, is not very popular with our group. I like cornmeal mush okay, but in Africa it is thickened with corn flour till you can actually cut it with a knife. Instead of *ugali*, we eat rice, beans, chapatti, and cabbage or chopped greens. One day when I'm on kitchen duty, Violet takes me out in a farmer's field and teaches me to cut the tender young leaves from the pumpkin plants which grow among the cornstalks. They make delicious cooked greens; whoever would have guessed. Everything is cooked with plenty of salt and oil for a long time. No subtle or spicy flavors here, only salt.

I've never been overly fond of potatoes, but when one of us discovers a source, I happily stuff myself with them just like everyone else. What a treat after so much rice. On the rare occasions that a villager kills a cow, we're told, the meat is shared with everyone in this small hamlet. I guess beef stew would make the *ugali* more palatable, but I never find out, as I'm not a meat-eater. Just once we have chicken.

Though chickens are running around everywhere, it's difficult to buy eggs because the owners prefer to let the eggs hatch. Except for the occasional banana, we have no fresh fruit until one day when I notice a kid sauntering by with a basket of hard unripe limes. They have been ordered by someone else, but eventually he brings some for us, which I squeeze by hand into real limeade, sweetened with honey. It hits the spot with everyone. I don't think we would have survived even that short time on such basic rations had not some of our group brought goodies which they generously shared — peanut butter, M&M's and other snacks.

African hospitality is famous and we try to reciprocate. Anyone observed in or near our big house is automatically invited to join us for a meal. Several evenings Steve invites one of the school faculty to talk to us on some aspect of politics or local customs. Once, three male teachers who live upstairs dine with us and stay for singing and dancing and silly games. It's a little embarrassing because they all sing so well, and we don't. Violet teaches us a song, "Humble yourself before the Lord" which has a catchy rhythm. She is a stalwart of the church choir.

At eight-thirty Sunday morning, wearing our African garb, we attend the fully packed church, men on one side, women on the other. An itinerant Swedish pastor preaches in Swahili. There's lots of singing and frequent ululating from women in the crowd. I would have called it yodeling. At the end, we all stand up front and introduce ourselves, one by one, with Steve making a short speech in Kiswahili about how glad we are to be here. The next day we discover that we had been expected to sing "Humble yourself" for the pleasure of the congregation. We hadn't realized that, and I'm sure our voices would have sounded mighty poor to that audience of such fine natural singers.

The beauty of the *Pommern* area and the voices raised in song are my favorite memories from Tanzania. During those frequent periods when the students and we Americans wait at the work site for instructions and supervision, we quickly run out of conversation, after "What is your name?" and "How old are you?" Later the kids get bold enough to ask me "Why do you live alone?" and "Why don't you find another husband?" Sooner or later, while Lois and I and some thirty to sixty students stand in the bright sun passing bricks, they spontaneously start singing. Sheer delight. I am convinced that all Africans are born with perfect pitch, and their harmonizing is infallible. Mormon Tabernacle Choir, watch out.

Trudging through far-reaching maize fields and down a shady aisle of tall eucalyptus trees to our worksite is a wonderful way to start the day. We greet the people we meet, saying *kamwene*, but their reply is usually *shikamoo*, a polite response to older people, appropriate for Lois and me. The green gently rolling countryside extends in all directions, topped with ever-changing cloud scenes. The red soil, usually muddy, coats my tennis shoes, layer on layer, till I wonder if I'll have to jettison them when I leave. But no, in *Dar-es-Salaam* the mud soaks off, and I'm wearing them happily now. We tend to look upon lack of electricity as a real hardship. But how else would we have seen the bright starry sky so clearly? And on the nights we have thunderstorms, we are treated to real sound and light shows.

One day Lois and I visit the home of Mercy's uncle, or "small father" as they say. We couldn't be more surprised to find that he is the big handsome tractor driver who had transported our student group way out in the country for a load of bricks a few days before. We have been told he is a "peasant"—pronounced *peezant*—but in this subsistence level hamlet, he is a prosperous exception, with a living compound of several buildings, including a large brand-new house for his family of five children. Three of the girls show us how to pound maize with a large mortar and pestle. Another surprise: he gets out a fancy Minolta camera and tripod to take our pictures. I am happy to again play mailman with letters he has written to his niece Mercy in *Dar-es-Salaam*; otherwise, it might take the postal service two weeks to deliver his mail.

Another day, Violet takes us to her home where we meet her mother, a skilled basket maker. Since I myself like to weave baskets, I'm fascinated by her demonstration, and buy one of the small shallow ones to remember her by. The grasses she uses are totally different from anything I've worked with in Florida, of course. Baskets, large and small, are traditional household containers, so much more beautiful than the garish plastic basins and buckets being used more and more.

As time goes on, our volunteer group shrinks. Will, who had trouble adapting to food or anything else, hops on a bus and heads for home after a few days. Peggy and Marta, tired of lack of accomplishment and unhappy with living conditions, leave to visit Mikumi Park for the last three days. We will collect them there on our way back to *Dar*. I enjoy working with Lois, who is nearer my age than the others. Also, she's had African experience doing graduate work in Ghana, so can give me a useful perspective on cultural characteristics here.

We end up scarcely eating dorm food the last couple of days, choosing instead to visit the "New Highlands Restaurant," a place smaller than its name, where we subsist on greasy fried potatoes and soft drinks. Local beer, either Tusker or Safari brand, isn't bad. Friday night we entertain about twenty-five guests with vast quantities of our staple cuisine. We may be bored with it but they are delighted, as rice is too costly for the average person. This is the time to bring out my packet of Florida postcards. They prove to be a welcome—if modest—gift for each guest.

When Saturday rolls around, we are packed up well before the Lutheran truck rolls up. Lo and Susan, after a holiday traveling around Tanzania, will be coming back to volunteer longer in *Pommern*, this time as teachers. Frankly, I can't imagine doing that after our rugged two weeks, but I admire their dedication. They move their possessions upstairs to our room, padlock the door and hope for the best. We've all "lost" innumerable possessions, mostly small items like caps, work gloves, or pens, while we've been here. If I owned as little as most Africans do, perhaps I would feel that visiting foreigners were fair game.

We're underway by eleven a.m.—not only our seven people but at least that many more Tanzanians, as usual. A free ride, after all. En route back, we con Steve into agreeing that we can stay at a hotel in *Iringa* rather than at the barren

Lutheran Center. This hotel seems like heaven to us, though it might qualify for a one-star rating in our country. The rain is teeming down as usual.

Next day, riding in a comfortable van which has come from *Dar* for us, we do a game drive through Mikumi, where the signs say "Take no liberties with game animals." The most offensive and ubiquitous creatures here are the tsetse flies, which invade our vehicle. Large and tenacious, they seem undaunted by insect repellent, and we have no open rooftop through which to wave them out. Here at last are the great vistas of savannah which I had always envisioned in East Africa. It being mid-day, we don't expect to spot lions. But look—up on two low branches of a large tree are two female lions stretched out having a siesta, languid paws hanging down. We drive squarely under them to get close-ups. Shortly thereafter, a sharp-eyed visitor notices another lion stalking through tall elephant grass near our roadway. He doesn't stop and pose for us, as the lions in the Masai Mara had often done.

After picking up our two missing volunteers, we head for *Dar-es-Salaam* and finally arrive at the truly luxurious Agip in time for a late dinner. What a bustling city it now seems. The next day, six of our group take a day trip by ferry to *Zanzibar*, the famous spice island, which I had visited earlier. Therefore I miss the scary experience that three of the women have while strolling on the beach. A handsome young African comes up to them, saying *Jambo Mama* and, pulling out a knife, proceeds to rob them. It happens very fast and then he vanishes. The loss of their passports and money not only delays their departure for home, supposedly the following day, but makes a most unhappy finale to their African experience. Our final dinner together in *Dar* is not as cheerful as it might have been. I guess I was just lucky on my excursion there.

Lois and I share a room for a couple more days in the capital city. When we leave a few pieces of worn clothing in the wastebasket before repacking and checking out, the hotel requires us to sign a statement saying that we deliberately discarded them. Obviously, they've learned to protect their staff from charges of thievery.

I read somewhere that "The best…travel encounters jolt us out of routine and reveal new attitudes and insights about ourselves… They keep our lives from becoming stale." That describes my East African adventures to a "T." No stale lives on this trip.

ZIMBABWE Bathing in the Zambezi

CHAPTER 5

1994
HIP HIP HIPPO SAFARI

Monkeys lurk nearby to gobble up what is left of our sandwich lunch before we slide our well-loaded canoes into the broad Zambezi River at *Chirundu* in Zimbabwe, one March day. Jeremy, our soft-spoken young blonde guide and leader, wastes little time teaching the nine of us how to handle our canoes. Debbie and Isabel are from Scotland, and six French family members make up the rest of the contingent, so of course I—the singleton—have the privilege of sharing Jeremy's canoe, which frequently leads our five-canoe expedition.

Here I am, on my first visit to Africa. After taking a safari in Kenya and working for three weeks in Tanzania, I've come to visit old friends who live in *Harare*, the modern capital of Zimbabwe. At their suggestion I fly to spectacular *Victoria Falls* for a couple of days before taking this Zambezi River excursion. A small plane gets me to *Hwange* and then to *Kariba* to join a Shearwater Expeditions safari. A three-hour drive the next morning takes us to the launching ramp for the river itself, to begin a new adventure. Had I gone on the Zambezi at

Vic Falls, we would have had world-class whitewater rafting, but here, farther east, the river is placid and offers far more game viewing—more my style. The French group drove here from *Harare*, a distance of some two hundred miles.

Although Jeremy spends most of his days on the Zambezi, the scene constantly changes, so an island he camped on two weeks ago may be virtually washed away now. He has to make quick decisions at every bend of the river, which has multiple channels and divergent branches. We are warned to be on constant lookout for stumps, sandbars, crocodiles and hippopotamuses. It keeps one on high alert and we do indeed encounter all of these.

Today is our longest unbroken spell of paddling—four hours in brutal afternoon sun. At five-thirty we pull onto a sandy island, wryly nicknamed "Twin Peaks" for its two barely noticeable slight slopes. Choices: I opt for a cozy little pop-up screened tent while the others, feeling mighty warm, choose ingenious mosquito net arrangements atop their sleeping bags right out on the sandy ground. The sunset over the scrubby horizon is awe-inspiring; then comes total darkness. Jeremy's candlelight dinner, complete with chilled wine, hits the spot, and we all hit the hay before nine, after surreptitious forays with flashlights into the near underbrush. I find that no matter how much water I drink—from the Zambezi River—my need to take shovel and bucket to find elusive privacy is rare, and that simplifies life.

Between the heat and the constant mooing snuffling sounds of the hippos which come ashore at night to graze, sleep does not come easily, tired as we are. We've been warned that the hippos will be foraging on our sandbar all night long, but not to worry. A full moon rises about midnight, bright as daylight. It seems no time at all till we are awakened at five-thirty for tea and cookies. We load canoes and are off before seven. Heading due east, the air is cool and we have a perfect view of the sun rising—I in particular, being in the lead canoe. The pattern is established; we stop at about eight-thirty for a huge breakfast of canned fruit, baked beans, bacon, scrambled eggs, bread and peanut butter. Although the French canoers initially look askance at the baked beans, I notice that everything is consumed with relish day after day.

Bernhard, from the French Embassy in *Harare*, is steady and reliable, paddling with his enthusiastic fourteen-year-old son Julian. His wife, Janou, and her visiting sister Michelle, share a canoe and occasionally have some difficulty staying in single file or changing course quickly when there's imminent danger. Michelle's daughter Florence, with husband Jean-Marc, often act as rear guard. Jean-Marc is adept in the water, having captained a sixty-foot yacht in the West Indies for years before moving to Paris. All of our band really pull their weight and cooperate in whatever needs doing. We quickly become a friendly and compatible team.

I am the luckiest, of course, to be canoeing with handsome Jeremy. Ah, if only I were younger. He is a native of Zimbabwe and has always lived here although it would be easy to take him for a Brit. Before independence in 1980, this was a British colony called Rhodesia, after all. Jeremy feeds us lots of information about birds and animals and trees as we go along, as well as river lore. By the time the trip is over, I'm amazed that my Field Card lists twenty-seven different birds I've spotted, although it is the darting kingfisher, brilliant blue, and the huge African fish eagle, something like our bald eagle, that I particularly remember.

Surprisingly, the first day of paddling didn't make my muscles ache, but eventually the unaccustomed exertion gets to my shoulders. It helps that I can lean on my paddle occasionally without making much difference in our progress. At times we can coast along languidly, but to navigate the tricky spots requires hard paddling and strict attention to Jeremy's instructions. When a blessed breeze arrives, the frisky water demands more effort. We've each been given a "bailing cup," but use it less for bailing than to dip up cooling drinks of river water. In all the countries I've visited, it's always been unwise to drink ordinary tap water until I got to *Harare*. And now this river water is equally potable, though somewhat murky when you're too close to the muddy shore.

Hippos are a constant concern. We're all supposed to be on the lookout for them, but more often than not, the hippo we novices think we're seeing turns out to be a tree stump. Of course Jeremy knows their favorite hangouts, and to warn them, he bangs frequently on the side of the canoe. If they're around, they'll surface to avoid the underwater sound waves, which hurt their ears. They like deep water, so our five canoes hug the river edges, but it's all too easy to get hung up on stumps there or be waylaid by overhanging trees. The Zambezi, seventeen hundred miles long, lies between Zambia and Zimbabwe. The number of safaris allowed on the river is strictly regulated. Today our course follows the high Zambian Escarpment, looming at our left, beautiful in its ever-changing light and shadow. What a surprise to see an occasional fisherman or a small village. We feel a rare sense of peace and privacy and stillness, even though we're never far from African humanity.

Slathered as we are with constant applications of sunscreen and minus any real bathing facilities, it's a delight to have a refreshing splash in the river late the second morning. We take no chances with crocodiles, which we have occasionally seen sunning themselves on the riverbanks. The canoes are lashed together in a rough protective arc near the sandy shore. The shallow water doesn't allow for a real swim but nobody complains. When canoeing, we all wear long-sleeved shirts and hats for protection. Since we must walk right into the river to board the canoes, shorts are in order, but on board we drape a big towel or sarong over our legs and feet to fend off the fierce sun.

After navigating treacherous "Stump Alley" successfully, we stop for a cold lunch at the first shady spot. Stretched out on mattresses, we read or rest during the midday heat before paddling another two hours later in the afternoon. The riverbed is so different at the next campsite that I feel quite like a hippo myself, trying to haul gear over the deep sucking mud. This time *three* tents go up. We all use insect repellent freely, but except at dusk I have no problem with mosquitoes, and not once do I see the large blood-sucking tsetse fly which transmits sleeping sickness. March must be the wrong — or right — season.

Our third day out is similar to the rest except that the river views are ever-changing and we paddle only till lunchtime. This island is steeper and wooded, more of a proper island instead of an overgrown sandbar. After a quiet afternoon of relaxation, we're thrilled to watch a small parade of elephants plod from our side over to Zambia just before the sun sets. We *all* use tents tonight. Thick trees overhead prevent us from seeing the usual spectacular Southern Cross and rising moon.

Several people have heard lions during our last two nights. That is why we always camp on islands; lions are not likely to swim across to seek us out. While hippos may graze near us and sound close enough to touch, in fact they are not aggressive except when a pair of males is competing for river territory or if a mother gets separated from her young and we're caught in between. The latter scenario almost happened to our canoe in a narrow channel on our final morning. A baby popped up just a paddle's length to my port side, its mother in slightly deeper water. We were in danger of running aground as we slithered close to the riverbank, but fortunately they both moved toward the deeper channel. In fact, people in the canoes behind didn't even see Baby Hippo, her ears and eyes surfaced so briefly so close to me. My private thrill.

Our four day safari seems just about the right length for me, but I still feel sad when *Mana Pools National Park* appears after only two hours on the river this last morning. The experience has been so removed from normal life and so satisfying that I hate to see it end. Is it possible we traversed only forty-two miles? On the other hand, to have a hot shower and be able to use makeup will feel good.

Being near any water is always soothing, but paddling such a tortuous riverine course keeps you guessing. What will be around the next bend? Which of the possible channels ahead should we take? (Thank you, Jeremy, for your experienced leadership. We would surely have gotten lost many times otherwise.) And then there's that element of danger, being so close to animals in the wild, that keeps the adrenaline flowing, and the antenna on high alert. The mystery, excitement and serenity of canoeing the Zambezi River will remain with me as I return to the hustle bustle of *Harare* city life for my final few days on the exotic continent of Africa.

BHUTAN Himalayan horizon

CHAPTER 6

1995
LAND OF THE THUNDER DRAGON

The mountains are calling to me. Although I grew up among the Green Mountains of Vermont, I have now lived a long while in the flatness of Florida. White sand is fine, but I yearn now to "lift up mine eyes unto the hills." Sequestered Bhutan, high in the Himalayas, appeals to my sense of exploration. Sometimes called a living Shangri La, Bhutan allows only three thousand tourists to visit each year, and I'm eager to be one of them.

For the past three winters I've been taking a two-to-three month overseas trip, always sticking to parts of the world where we had lived on assignments with the US Foreign Service. Now I'm ready to venture slightly farther afield, but with assistance. I've never taken a package tour, preferring to free-lance my way around. But since this is new territory for me, I sign up for a Bhutan tour which will follow a short visit to my beloved *Madras*, India. I know this will be quite pricey, but it becomes even more so shortly before I leave Florida. I'm informed that I am the only person on this particular tour, so I must either cancel out or pay a single supplement. Too late to cancel, I'm off on a costly private excursion. I don't even think of how it will feel to lack companionship en route.

The tiny kingdom of Bhutan, about the size of New Hampshire and Vermont combined, lies tucked away northeast of India and south of Tibet. On a bright clear day early in March, I fly from *New Delhi* to *Paro*, the only airport in Bhutan, on Druk Air, the national airline. The mountains are white with snow when we land in *Paro*, which is in one of the few valleys in this high Himalayan country. My private guide, handsome young Tashi, wearing his native dress, a red striped robe, welcomes me at the airport, bearing the sign of his tour agency, "Etho Metho." That name sounds like a comical jingle to me until I learn that it means rhododendron in the local Dzongkha language. I learn to say *tashi delek* to one and all, a universal greeting. It seems as though half the men in Bhutan are named *Tashi*, meaning *auspicious*.

In my brightly painted hotel bungalow, the mural over the bathtub mimics the outside scene, a postcard perfect view of Taktsang, a monastery perched high on a sheer cliff across the *Paro* valley. Taktsang—Tiger's Lair—is so-called because its location was determined by the Buddhist Lama Padmasambava, also known as Guru Rinpoche. Legend has it that he was dropped in this precarious spot by the tigress that flew him here from Tibet. He is revered for bringing Buddhism, the national religion, to Bhutan. I'll see more statues of Padmasambava in temples than those of the Buddha himself.

Our very first day we take a muleback ride, followed by a tiring hike up a steep trail, to visit gravity-defying Taktsang. The sluggish mule never picks up his pace no matter how authoritatively I say *chuh-chuh* as instructed. Looking across a deep ravine at the picturesque hermitage, which still houses a few monks, I'm busy taking photos when Tashi warns me not to step back. It seems that I'm standing on the very spot, with a sheer drop-off behind me, where an eighty-five year old

American tourist had recently lost his life. He unwittingly stepped backward and fell to his death. Enchanted by the spectacular surroundings, I wonder if at his age this might not be so bad a place and way to die. Still, I am careful to stay away from the precipice, and my knees are really shaky as we make our way back down to the trailhead.

We also visit the museum in an ancient watchtower— *dzong*—the first of many, and other historical sites around *Paro*. Two days later, I am impressed at how skillfully our driver, roguish Kinley, navigates the forty-five miles—two hours—into *Thimphu*, the capital. The road is steep and has a constant series of serpentine curves. Little do I realize that during most of the next three weeks in Bhutan we will traverse ever steeper, ever more hair-raising roads. I've always found it easy to snooze during extended car rides, but not in this mountainous country.

Thimphu is the only real city in all of Bhutan, although it has only forty thousand residents. As I notice how people greet each other on the street, I realize that it's really an overgrown village, with but one traffic cop. With a population of just one and a quarter million in the entire country, the Bhutanese are very proud of their nation, their culture, their handsome king. Bhutan has learned from the desecration of the environment in neighboring Nepal. Not only is there a strict limit on the number of foreign visitors, no television is received here—a deliberate policy to keep outside influences at bay. However, Bhutan is a poor country, mostly agricultural, so the government, needing dollars, determines the daily charge for tourists. No way can you visit on the cheap and just wander around on your own. No hippies allowed, as in Nepal.

We're on a hillside overlooking *Thimphu*, admiring the mountain views surrounding us, with dozens of Buddhist prayer flags flapping wildly in the wind. Such bright flags are ubiquitous, strung up on private rooftops, at monastery entrances or, as here, on tall poles, sending prayers heavenward. Two modern cars suddenly zoom up and stop nearby. Out jump two young beauties, dressed in form-fitting Western clothes, one of them smoking a cigarette. After talking flirtatiously with the two young men in the other car, they all speed off again. Tashi identifies one of the girls as the king's sister-in-law. It seems to me more like a Hollywood scene than what I would expect to see in this unspoiled country. Forty-year old King Jigme has four wives who are all sisters, plus four sons and six daughters. He is much revered.

Unless you're in the royal family, apparently, native dress is supposed to be worn by all. For the men, it is a kimono-like robe, calf-length, called a *gho,* worn with knee-high hose. Often these are a bright striped or plaid weave, on other occasions more formal dark gray. A white shirt with extra long sleeves makes a broad cuff when folded up several inches over the sleeves of the *gho.* Women's long gowns, called *kiras,* are pinned at the shoulder with a large brooch; a broad sash—*kabney*—completes the outfit. The versatile *kabney* is often used by both men and women for a baby sling. Out in the country, we see backstrap looms at many houses, where the women of the family weave rich colored woolen fabrics. Also out in the country I notice many young men, especially teenagers, wearing blue jeans instead of the *gho,* despite the rules.

When we pack up to drive from *Thimphu* to *Punakha,* I look behind me in our four-wheel drive Land Cruiser, and there is a new face. "I'm the chef," announces Sonam, then promptly falls asleep. So here I am, accustomed to traveling modestly and alone, now escorted by an entourage of three—private guide, private driver and now my own cook. It just doesn't feel natural. Actually, we won't need Sonam for another week, when we'll have a three day camping experience in and around *Tashiyangtse,* in the easternmost part of Bhutan. However, public transport is so minimal that coming with us now is the best way for him to get to where we'll need him.

We arrive in the old capital of *Punakha* just in time for its annual *tsechu* or festival. Here are plenty of European tour groups, plus thousands of Bhutanese of all ages gathered from near and far. Amidst their hard lives, a *tsechu* is a welcome opportunity to dress in their finest clothes, drink a little, flirt a little, and equally important, observe religious rituals and dance-dramas. We have to climb steep outer stairs with no handrails to enter the inner courtyard of the *dzong* where a range of activities takes place over many hours. There's plenty of excitement and noise—firecrackers, drums, deafening horns, weirdly masked dancers. I wish I had worn earplugs. My head aches when I finally escape, even without tasting from the huge vat of barley beer.

After *Punakha*, we wend our way eastward across this mountainous country, with nightly stops in *Tongsa*, *Bumthang, Mongar* and eventually *Tashigang*. Everywhere we visit *dzongs*, the center of activity for each village. Built as ancient fortresses, the gold-roofed *dzong* is now used partly for town business—judges, licensing and such—and partly as temple monasteries. This admixture which seems strange to an American, perfectly epitomizes how completely Buddhism, the national religion, is tied to the administration of the country. The distinctive architecture—painted in bright reds and golds—is also seen in private homes, only less opulent. Some *dzongs* serve as museums as well.

Bucolic *Bumthang* valley is a totally different scene. In this pastoral setting are beehives; herds of cattle produce delicious cheeses made under Swiss supervision. Bhutan is an agricultural country where cheese is a staple food, but their cheese is quite unlike the Swiss version. Earlier, we stopped at a farmer friend of Tashi's to get some. For less than one US dollar, he bought four fresh rounds, each one weighing perhaps one and a half pounds. Their cheese is crumbly like Feta but not salty, and is typically melted in the national dish, *emedatzi*, which is very hot and full of chilis, eaten with rice.

Delicious! At this time of year, few vegetables are available, but ingenious Sonam presents cabbage and cauliflower in numerous tasty ways. He cooked for a previous king. My favorite dish is the round Tibetan steamed dumpling called *momo*, served at most of our hotel buffet dinners. The filling is usually beef or pork but may also be cheese or veggies. Even without much variety, I eat very well indeed.

The *Paro* airport is 8,500 feet high, and I climbed slowly, huffing and puffing, to 10,000 feet at *Taktsang* on my first day. We are now crossing ever higher passes till we reach 12,045 feet at *Thromseng La*. Snow, which we've seen under the trees near the road as well as on high peaks, is quite deep here. A large Swedish tour bus ahead of us has gotten stuck, completely blocking the narrow road. Even with our four-wheel drive Land Cruiser, we can't continue till we help shovel them out. We'll be seeing these Swedish tourists later at our camping area.

This east-west "Lateral Highway" from *Thimphu* to *Tashigang* is a real engineering achievement. It is three hundred and fifty miles long, mostly two lanes, fortunately with only light traffic, especially east of the highest pass, where we are now. To carve it out of the mountainside took ten years, starting in 1965, plus another ten years to pave it. Altogether about two hundred and fifty workers lost their lives on the project, mostly Nepalis and Indians. Even now, the road maintenance crews, I'm told, are not Bhutanese. I ride in front with Kinley, while Tashi and Sonam lounge in the back with the gear. When I can tear my eyes away from the sharp hairpin turns in the road, I look up at steep wooded hillsides. After we navigate the next switchback, I find myself looking downward to rushing gorges far below, with no protective guardrails. One can hardly doze off in these circumstances, nor do I recommend this highway for the faint-hearted. We cover eighteen miles per hour on average.

Tashigang is the farthest village to the east before we veer north. This is off the usual tourist track. The next three hours are the hairiest travel so far, with several heart-stopping near misses. It's lucky that there's so little traffic to worry about; the steep drop-offs take all my attention. I'm surprised to see young Bhutanese girls crushing rock for the road crews. We're following a tributary of the Brahmaputra River to the town of *Tashiyangtse*, which is dominated by the huge 12th century stupa—prayer pagoda—of Chorten Kora. We're here because of another *tsechu*, and again throngs of pilgrims have traveled long distances to worship.

The Drogpa people of this area are semi-nomadic yak herders, distinguished by their round black yak-hair caps with five small "pigtails" sticking out from the sides. Their hair seems even blacker than I've seen yet, and their high cheekbones make them look Oriental. The men wear turquoise earrings and daggers in their belts. The festival, although Buddhist, includes elements of the pre-Buddhist— Bon— religion. Worshippers walk many clockwise circuits around the domed stupa to show their devotion. Even fun-loving Tashi admits to having circled it twenty times on our first evening here.

This is the first of three places where we camp out in tents instead of staying in the ornate government tourist lodges. Since the weather is mild, it's a pleasant change in the routine, and my sleeping bag is quite adequate. The winds from Tibet were bitter in the west and I had a hard time keeping warm in unheated lodges, despite extra blankets. The Swedish tour group with their many red tents creates a small village near us in this big field. As a solo traveler, I relish their sociability. We're above a rushing river which roars in my dreams all night. One night Tashi arranges for village women to dance for us to the sound of a local flute. An impromptu performance, lubricated by barley beer—*chang*—it is fun and goes on late into the night, dancers and viewers alike relaxed and noisy.

Now it's time to reverse directions. On our way back across the country we visit *Gangtey*, winter headquarters for the rare endangered black-necked cranes. We hear they have all just flown off to Tibet, but we get up very early and navigate a marshy field till sharp-eyed Kinley sees three of them up ahead. For every delicate step we take toward them, they in turn retreat from us. So my pictures are no good, but I'm glad to have seen them. We've also seen hoopoes, laughing thrushes, and iridescent blue birds. In the east I got my first view of an occasional big lumbering black yak grazing lazily on the hillside, and sometimes a family of monkeys sat by the road and observed us driving by. In that milder climate, corn was being dried at the edge of the road, and tall rhododendron and poinsettias brightened up the scenery. Subsistence farming—corn and barley—is the lot of the Bhutanese who live in the valleys.

Cavernous *Gangtey* guesthouse is right adjacent to the monastery. Off and on during the day we observe the lively young monks, released from their studies, throwing darts. Archery is the national sport of Bhutan, and we've seen it everywhere. I'm not sure why, but archery is forbidden for monks, so we see them playing soccer or native sports instead. I catch a glimpse of a blond American woman who is staying in *Gangtey* for four months to study meditation. Since I can hardly sleep from the cold myself, even with flannel sheets and wearing most of my clothes, I have to admire her dedication.

Monasteries formerly provided the only education in Bhutan, and the most promising son in each family was expected to become a monk. Nowadays, public education is rapidly improving under the direction of the current king and with assistance from the UN and various international non-governmental agencies. Everywhere we go, we see schools overflowing with both boys and girls in school uniform, styled like native dress. Therefore the influence of religious education has waned, and the standards of it as well.

It is more than two weeks since we left *Thimphu*. When we return, late in March, the scent of spring is in the air. Trees are leafing out; there are blossoms on cherry, magnolia, forsythia. We have seen rhododendron bushes blooming throughout the country, as well as whole hillsides and fields covered with a lavender blanket of primula flowers. Not only that, *Thimphu* seems quite citified after our being in such rustic surroundings for so long. Outside the capital there is a sign: "Pot Hole Reporting Center." At a checkpoint reporting stop en route to *Paro*, I see a tiny building offering "Espresso Coffee." Civilization indeed.

In the temples I've seen beautiful *thankas*, so it's interesting to visit the government sponsored Thanka Painting and Maskmakers School and watch the student artists at work. In fact, I get carried away and buy four *thankas*, each illustrating a typical Buddhist theme, such as the Tree of Life or a mandala. The *thanka* is a kind of inspirational painting or embroidered work of art hung in Buddhist temples and devout households. Except for handmade paper and weavings, I've not found many other handicrafts to bring home from Bhutan.

At the National Library, Khenpo Phuntsok Tashi is my delightful guide. It happens that he was born in one of the villages we visited in the east, but at age twelve he was sent to study in *Darjeeling* in India. Later he studied in *Varanasi* and other parts of India before finally being ordained as a Buddhist monk and assigned to the National Library, where his warm gentle personality and language skills make him an excellent guide for foreign visitors. He's even traveled recently to Germany and Scandinavia.

Much to my surprise and pleasure, Khenpo invites me to his home for dinner this evening. I don't expect a burgundy-robed monk to drive me in his little car to his hillside home, but that's what happens. Khenpo is tall and rather large, in his early thirties. He has a round gentle face and warm eyes behind dark-rimmed glasses. Because he's been recently tonsured, he wears a dark red knit cap to keep his head warm. Various family members, his siblings and their children, overflow the modest home. We share a simple but tasty meal together, and he shows me his small meditation room. I assume it's also his bedroom, full of photographs and memorabilia. In general I have found Bhutanese people to be friendly and attractive, but Khenpo's hospitality this evening has given a welcome added dimension to my views of this country.

Now it is back to *Paro* for one night before I leave Bhutan for Nepal and Tibet, from one high country to two more. I wonder if my faithful retinue of driver, guide and cook are as glad to say goodbye to me as I am to them. They did their jobs well, but traveling in solitary splendor—with attendants—is not my preferred style. I've never wanted to be a prima donna, and this trip has reinforced that sentiment.

Visually stunning as Bhutan is, it doesn't seem quite real in some way. Is that because of the sparse population? Or the government controlled lifestyle? It has a Rip Van Winkle quality which I come to realize only after reaching *Kathmandu*, where I can read the daily English language newspaper and watch television. I wonder how long before outside influences will drag this small gem of an ancient nation into the modern world. Anyway, I'll always be able to say, "I saw it way back when...."

VIETNAM Sugar cane vendor

CHAPTER 7

1998
HIGH ON HANOI

"Why would you want to go to *North* Vietnam?" I was asked more than once before I returned to *Hanoi* for the third time recently.

My first views of Vietnam during a month of touring in 1996 whetted my appetite so much that I wanted to see more, particularly in the lesser-visited North. I was impressed with Dr. Canh, who led me on a trek seeking the elusive langur, a primate, in the rainforests near the Chinese border. He promptly suggested that I could teach English on my next visit. That is just what I did, and those two months were so enjoyable that here I am in 1998, ready to return to the Institute for Ecology and Biological Resources in *Hanoi*.

But first, I'm touring a bit with ex-daughter-in-law Vicki and niece Margaret. Vicki grew up overseas, and I already know that we travel well together, but this is Margaret's first foray to an exotic destination. She said recently, "You know, Dorothy, some day I'd like to travel with you." So here she is.

The Mekong Delta south of *Saigon*, famous as it is, is new to me. Vicki and I have just spent a day on the Mekong River near *Luang Phabang* in Laos, and now we are on a one day tour to *My Tho*, two hours south of *Ho Chi Minh City* and thirty miles from the sea. Our little tour group piles into a ferry boat to cross the wide brown river to *Unicorn Island*. We wander among the tropical fruit groves and are given samples of small sweet bananas, pineapple, papaya, sapodilla and longan. Delicious!

Then, via tipsy small boats we're poled through narrow backwaters to *Coconut Monk Island*, named for a Buddhist monk who supposedly subsisted solely on coconuts for twenty some years. Nowadays the coconuts grown here are processed into a very sweet chewy taffy that is popular throughout Vietnam. In deference to the labor-intensive making of this confection, which we watch, we buy packets to munch on. My dentist would be horrified.

Back in *Ho Chi Minh City*—still called *Saigon* by most people—we hire *cyclos* to ride around and get an overview of the city, stopping to tour the Unification Palace and the Xa Loi Pagoda. For eighty-three cents per hour, we're pedaled from behind in these three-wheeled pedicabs. I've ridden in plenty of pedicabs in other countries, but sitting up front, exposed this way, is scary, even on a Sunday when traffic congestion is less.

Almost as soon as Margaret arrives, she discovers a small music shop where she falls in love with a beautiful Vietnamese "zither," complete with inlaid mother-of-pearl decoration. This will surely be the most exotic musical instrument among the collection of banjos, dulcimers, etc. in their New England home. Carefully wrapped, the fragile instrument goes with her on each leg of our travels. Exploring at huge covered Ben Thanh Market, we ogle the wide range of merchandise, but buy little. There will be plenty of opportunities to shop later on. But we do get pedicures off in a little corner, for the sheer novelty of it, and because it costs each of us less than one US dollar.

Near the Cambodian border, west of *Saigon,* is the village location of the *Cao Dai Holy See.* This unique admixture of Buddhism, Catholicism and other world religions seems to flourish in this area, although organized religion now plays but a small role throughout the country. Four masses a day are held at six and twelve, morning and evening, every day of the year. White-robed worshippers, men and women on separate sides of the cavernous cathedral, kneel and chant to the accompaniment of stringed instruments, surrounded by brilliantly carved pillars. Outside, the formal gardens contain many contrived topiary animals worthy of a Walt Disney display.

Now it's time to leave the Giant Dragon, our *Saigon* hotel, for the one-hour flight north to *Danang.* Spread out on a peninsula between the Han River and the Bay of Danang, this city has a notable museum of statuary from the Champa period, but little else of particular interest. Dapper Mr. Louis volunteers to be our guide at the museum, which reminds me of South India with its extensive collection of Hindu statuary from the 4th to 15th centuries. He arranges onward transport for us to *Hue* by way of *Hoi An,* with a chauffeur friend. It seems to us that we hear more English and more French spoken in *Danang* than in *Saigon.* And I'm amazed to see women of all ages smoking cigarettes here, on the street, in restaurants, everywhere. Later, we learn that Vietnamese women rarely smoke except in *Danang.*

But first we are headed for *Hoi An,* the highlight of my 1996 visit to Vietnam. Our driver, Mr. Hai, worked for two years in Czechoslovakia, and another driver, Mr. Anh, had "technical training" in *Leningrad* for five years. And here I had thought that it was only the highly educated Vietnamese, like my Institute students, who had been sent to the Soviet bloc countries for advanced study. Watching out the window we see mostly *padi* fields, with men and women busily planting rice, protected from the sun by their long sleeves and woven conical hats. Although the road follows the coast, we see very few birds, either songbirds or shorebirds. They have been shot for food over many years, we're told.

Hoi An is an enchanting mix of architecture and different cultural influences from the days when it was a center for Southeast Asian commerce three hundred years ago. We walk over the famous scarlet Japanese Covered Bridge, which was built to separate the Japanese and Chinese quarters of the town. It bears little resemblance to a New England covered bridge. Cars are banned in the old quarter, so one can roam freely from one or another Chinese assembly hall to various classical merchant homes, many still inhabited but open to visitors.

Shops and restaurants have a peculiar charm as well. On a whim I look for sandals in a shoe shop but don't find my size. The next day, the same shopkeeper flies out to nab me as I wander by, and proceeds to show me a newly made duplicate pair in my exact size. How can I resist buying them, especially since they cost all of four dollars? Vicki and Margaret are as impressed with the local specialty dish, *cao lau*, as I was two years ago. In fact, we enjoy this unusual soupy noodle dish for lunch so much that we have it again for an early supper before departing.

Driving north to the ancient capital of *Hue*, we stop for a look-see and picture-taking at *Hai Van* — Ocean Cloud — *Pass*. But the swarms of young vendors who attach themselves like leeches, pushing postcards and overpriced souvenirs at us, hasten our departure. In *Hue* we hire a boat to take us up the Perfume River — in name if not aroma — to the Thien Mu Pagoda and the Minh Mang and Gia Long tombs. This last destination is our favorite, walking for twenty minutes through rural countryside to the deserted tumbledown buildings of this early 19th century king. We're accompanied much of the way by chattering young girls who hold our hands while practicing their English and French — "tres jolie" — and even sing to us in Vietnamese and French. "Frere Jacques," of course.

On my first trip in 1996 I took the overnight Reunification Express train from *Hue* to *Hanoi*. This time it's a one-hour flight on a Vietnam Air Fokker-70 aircraft, along with many French tourists. We're spending our entire final week together in and around this elegant capital city.

Hanoi, with its many lakes and broad tree-lined streets, has far more charm than more modern *Saigon*, but it is busy and noisy, especially in the thousand-year-old Ancient Quarter. There is a medieval flavor here, with each block specializing in different products, such as silks, or metalware, or books. I wonder how long before the old "tube houses" will be replaced by modern high-rises. We might call them row houses. Their narrow street frontage is due to an ancient taxation system, whereby the tax was levied according to the width of the building at front. They could extend back a long way, though, and some even had courtyards in back. The living quarters are usually above the shop space, as evidenced by laundry hanging on upper balconies.

We enjoy an overnight getaway to scenic *Halong Bay*, with its myriad outcropping islets. The limestone *karst* looming out of the bay make for exquisite pictures, and it's hard to resist taking just one more, again and again, in the mist, in the sun, from all angles. A magical scene.

Since we three are vegetarian, but eat seafood, ordering restaurant meals can be tricky, even when we explain our food restrictions. One lunch time we're enjoying a highly recommended dish which involves rolling various raw shredded veggies and an omelet into thin rice paper wrappers. Dipped into a special sauce, it's deliciously unusual. But then we ask the waiter what the sauce consists of, and it turns out to include minced quail. No longer so appealing.

Although I am staying on here to teach again, the final day of our two weeks as a threesome finally arrives, and we walk around *Hanoi's* central lake, Hoang Kiem, in the early morning. We splurge on a special brunch of fresh juicy mango, yogurt and croissants at a patisserie near the Diamond Hotel before heading for the airport. Oh yes, and a young lad shines our shoes for twenty-five cents each as we eat. That's how these street kids keep themselves alive, that and selling packets of postcards at every busy street corner.

I hate to say goodbye to Vicki and Margaret, we have had such fun. They had not known each other before this but got along like old friends. I sort of thought they would. They're ideal travelers—curious, adaptable and tall. Here in this land of petite women and wiry men, it is fun for me to walk around flanked by two foreigners who attract so much attention. We share many laughs and taste treats. I am reminded that one always sees a familiar place with new eyes when traveling with people for whom it is virgin territory. Their perspective refreshes your own.

I'm pleased that Vicki and Margaret are also enchanted with Vietnam, the beauty of its coast and mountains, and the warmth of its people. For many Americans, Vietnam means only war. That tragic war which had so divided both our country and theirs is far more draining to us twenty years later than to the Vietnamese. They call it "the American war," and say, "We are fundamentally optimistic people; we don't forget but simply move ahead." An inspiring attitude.

Now I am ready to move over to the Institute to assume a different role. We came out here a few days ago to meet Dr. Sung, the Director, smiling efficient Dr. Canh, and my other friends from last year. We were served fresh mango and tea, and shown around the grounds of this government scientific facility. I learned that I would be staying in my same simple room in the official Guesthouse on the Institute grounds. I am volunteering my time and services, but the Institute provides my accommodation.

After I settle in, it turns out that I'll be teaching six classes a day. It is good to see familiar faces and to be welcomed with such enthusiasm. The Institute, a government scientific research facility, has no language program or teachers, but these experts are aware of how important English is in the international scientific community. Whether zoologists, entomologists, soil technologists, or graduate degree candidates, they prove to be bright, responsive and enthusiastic. Their exposure to English-speaking foreigners is very limited. They are eager to take full advantage of our small daily classes, and I am frequently invited on sightseeing expeditions or to visit one of their homes. Thus, while they are getting practice speaking English, I am getting informal close-up time with them and their families, a rare inside view for an outsider.

With no curriculum to follow, I have to be creative at planning lessons that are pertinent, giving the students practice in speaking, listening and a little reading and writing. It helps that classes are so small, four to seven students at most, sitting around a conference table. We never know when one or another of them will have to be away doing field work. This year they've asked for more practice in writing, which means more "homework" for me as well. It is not always easy to keep a straight face when hearing them read their work in class. Perhaps my most memorable quote is from one of my best students who grew up in a farm family, and says that his "father died at age sixty-three of high pleasure." Can you figure out what he really meant? (Blood pressure is often called simply "pressure," and we know how Asian accents get "r" and "l" interchanged.)

Another student, tall Miss Ngo Anh Dao, aged twenty-four, speaks French better than English—though that's not bad—and will leave soon for the University of Montreal on a full scholarship from the Canadian Government to do ecological research for her PhD. Petite Dr. (Mrs.) Dang Thi An is the only female department head. A biochemist, she studied for six years in the USSR, has two teen-age sons and likes gardening. Smiling Mr. Phan Van Mach is a hydro-biologist who likes music. He often helps cook for his ten-year-old son because his wife works long hours teaching English at a private school. One Sunday I go with her to an open-air market to shop for the lunch which we all eat together at their home.

Somebody introduces me to feisty Mrs. Ngoc, from whom I'm hoping to learn a little Vietnamese. Although I quickly give up on that idea, she volunteers to escort me on forays around town. My diet is much better this year, both from purchased foodstuffs—soup mixes and peanut butter—and from eating occasionally at a nearby family restaurant that she has recommended. They have no printed menu, but Mrs. Ngoc has told them of my tastes, so I merely point at those prepared dishes that look appealing. Although I don't eat meat, I can get a bountiful meal there of four or five dishes—greens, rice, veggie stews, sometimes fish—for about fifty cents or less. Food from street vendors doesn't tempt me because the national dish is *pho*, a noodle soup with a beef base, which I dislike. In fact, I'm surprised that, unlike in Thailand, beef is such a common ingredient in Vietnamese cuisine. The rest of my meals are from the limited menu at the Guesthouse; it's so convenient. Rarely are there any other guests staying here.

The jar of American peanut butter from a downtown shop sits open on my desk. I have enjoyed it on crackers several times, but today for the first time I notice the inside of the red plastic cover, with its impressed logo: *Sarasota FL Sun Plastics*. Am I dreaming or am I really sitting in *Hanoi* eating Louisiana peanut butter out of a container manufactured in my home town of *Sarasota*? Pinch me.

Perhaps Dr. Sung thinks that I'm getting restless, because he virtually insists that I go on an excursion to Ba Be National

Forest for a few days. My classes get a holiday while I join a group of eighteen Vietnamese foresters from all over the country for this segment of their training course. Ba Be means Five Lakes, and it is located two hundred and forty kilometers north of *Hanoi*. It takes us more than eight hours in a jeep, including a leisurely beery lunch en route. No matter how small the hamlet, every village we pass through has at least two familiar signs: *Photocopy* and *Karaoke*.

Fortunately, the foresters speak a smattering of English, and three of them latch onto this opportunity to practice their English with me every free moment. I might have anticipated this. For our two nights here I am housed in a cottage with the only woman in the class; slim Miss Chuong is one of the few mature Vietnamese women I've met who is unmarried.

Ba Be, established as a National Forest in 1992, is rich with hundreds of species of flora, animal and fish. In the cool morning mist we ride on skiffs around the finger lakes, stopping occasionally to explore caves or scramble on rocky trails to view secluded beauty spots. The following day we split into small teams to visit nearby farms. The idea is to enlist the help of local people in protecting the natural riches of the forest, but we can often hear the sound of saws, so I suspect the riches of the forest are considered fair game for public use. I seriously doubt that any of these nice forestry officials are very effective in preventing the poaching, and may even be guilty of selling plants or animals from their domains themselves.

But for me it is a rich opportunity to visit local homes and observe their rural lifestyles. Some are Hmong, others Thai ethnic minority. The children attend school three kilometers away, either morning or afternoon sessions. One head of household is a motor mechanic, one a carpenter; the others are farmers. The houses are simple, consisting of one large all-purpose room with dirt or concrete floor. Then there is a small back room for cooking, and overhead rafters for storage space. Most have radios but no TVs. Walls are decorated with family photos and glossy calendar pages. We are served tiny cups of tea or sometimes local wine. I am as much an object of curiosity to my hosts as they and their children are to me.

After Vietnam's long history of feudalistic oppression, it is impressive to see pervasive egalitarianism. The drivers are always included in our meals and all other activities and are treated respectfully. Everybody pitches in and helps with baggage or running errands. At the Institute I sense respect, but no undue apple-polishing of the Director and his deputy, who are elected by the staff. I realize that without knowing the language, I may miss subtle "class" distinctions that exist.

Back in Hanoi, after another day's jeep ride, it's good to have electricity twenty-four hours a day and hot water. My students all seem to own TVs but no automobiles, even the senior officials. Here in the city, the only cars appear to be tourist vans or office or government cars. Most people get around by bicycle, or if they can afford it, by motorbikes. I ride on the back of my students' mopeds many times, minus any helmet. In fact, I explore Hanoi primarily via motorcycle "taxis," always bargaining over the charge before starting out. That might be called living dangerously.

Much as I like *Hanoi*, it's not due to the weather. Since it's now winter, the skies are almost always gray, with frequent cold rain. As a Florida sun worshipper, I might prefer *Hanoi* in the summer, except that it gets extremely hot, I'm told, and air conditioning is rare except in tourist hotels. Since the Institute is on spacious grounds on the outskirts of *Hanoi*, it provides me a real oasis from the busy streets and markets in the heart of the city.

This final week of teaching, my classes get smaller as various scientists leave on research projects. Those who remain get sentimental, as do I, at my coming departure. Now, three of my younger students, in their 20s, have chosen to accompany me to the airport in the official Institute van.

When they ask me a bit about my Florida life, I dig out my driver's license to show them. I'll never forget the look of amazement on their faces when I refer to having a car—my own car—which I myself drive. We all thought we had come to know each other quite well over the months, but this casual conversation exposes the vast difference between their life in *Hanoi* and my life in the United States.

TUNISIA Edge of the Sahara

CHAPTER 8

2000
CARPETS, CAMELS AND ROMAN COLUMNS

This is the year I am going to concentrate on Mediterranean countries, a real switch for me from my usual Pacific and South Asian locales. Rarely do I go to an unfamiliar country totally on my own, and I admit to some trepidation on this first visit to an Arab country, Tunisia.

I want to book my *Tunis* accommodations, which I chose from a guidebook, before leaving Florida. With only a hotel phone number—no website or e-mail—and my minimal French language, I enlist the help of a French-speaking friend to make arrangements by phone. Sure enough, the modest three-star Carlton Hotel is expecting me when I arrive. I may be adventuresome, but I would not want to land with no idea where I was to lay down my head. I quickly orient myself and report in at the office of Carthage Tours. I've signed up for one of their excursions three days from now, so I have time to explore *Tunis* at leisure, all on my own.

Wandering the broad main Avenue Habib Bourguiba and smaller side streets, I happen to find the government tourism office where I get free maps. I also scope out an internet facility and some appealing restaurants. The streets are bustling with both men and smartly dressed women, but the cafes are patronized almost entirely by men. Most Tunisians wear the traditional long *jellabah* robe over their normal clothes, and men often wear a fez on their heads. In desert areas you see the practical *keffiyah* headdress, a very large woven square held in place by a decorative thong, practical for protection from the sandy winds. Cigarette smoking is common, even by women. I'm familiar with the European cheek-to-cheek greeting, but here it is often repeated several times after the initial handshake. Does that indicate simple friendliness or have some hidden ritualistic meaning?

My first adventure comes as I'm heading for the *medina*—the old Arab quarter—a short walk from the hotel. A large self-confident man sidles up to me, speaking good English. He says he's a security man at the "English Embassy" and has a sister who's married to an American and is a US citizen. If all that were true, he would know that it is the *British*—not *English*—Embassy. Despite my skepticism, I allow him to lead me to a large carpet salesroom not far inside the market area. He discreetly vanishes after delivering me there. I'm enchanted with the vast array of weavings, enough so that I end up bargaining for and buying three elegant twelve-inch carpet squares. Back at the hotel, I wonder *How could I have done that, and so early on in the trip? How will I tote them around for the next few weeks?* It's out of character for me to be so impetuous, but upon reflection I'm not sorry, because they will make very special gifts.

Later that day I have some anxious moments. It is early evening and I am walking along the wide central boulevard when a large crowd of noisy young men erupts from the opposite side. Is it a coup? Or a political demonstration? I'm frank to admit that I picked up my pace, turning quickly into a side street where I had earlier chosen a restaurant. But the ever-larger throng also turns, until it is right behind me. I duck with relief into the safety of the café and ask the waiter what exactly is going on. He laughingly informs me that these are happy fans celebrating the victory of Tunisia over Nigeria in a pan-African soccer tournament. Their cheering dies away as they surge past and continue their revelry.

As I orient myself to this new Muslim world, I'm learning about their food. My favorite dish is a savory *tajine*, slow cooked in a distinctive peaked clay pot. You might compare it to a pot roast, but the variety of spices, olives, even fruits added to the basic meat and vegetables raises the ingredients to a zesty succulence that no American pot roast could match. The tall pyramid-shaped lid traps the steam during the long simmering. The word *tajine* refers to the earthenware vessel as well as to the food. And then there's *briq*, phyllo-type dough encasing an egg or tuna fish, messy to eat but delicious. Salads are usually pungent with fennel. A bowl of olives and a tiny cup of strong syrupy mint tea are the first thing you're always served, but I can't drink much of the tea because it keeps me awake at night. Of course the robust espresso coffee is good, and the pastries are all loaded with honey.

What should I do on my final open day here? The tour office suggests a visit to the Roman ruins at *Dougga*, sixty miles southwest of *Tunis*. First I take a taxi to Bab Saadoun, the city gate which serves as a bus terminal, where I am to get a *louage* to *Dougga*. A *louage* is an unscheduled taxi which goes on a set route as soon as it has five passengers. What a noisy scene, with the drivers calling out their destinations to drum up business. I board my vehicle, grateful that there is one other woman passenger. The three men keep up a running conversation in Arabic with the handsome driver, I suspect largely about me.

We travel through rolling countryside of orchards and sheep, with donkeys the only other traffic, for one-and-a-half hours. At that point I am dropped off in front of a coffee shop amidst a small cluster of homes. It doesn't look much like

Roman ruins to me. A young man leisurely finishes his coffee before offering to drive me a couple of miles away to the actual site of *Dougga*. We are in *Dougga Nouvelle* here, a village created in the 1950s when the government, realizing the importance of protecting the site, removed the residents' houses from among the ancient ruins.

This is the first of many historic remains I'll be seeing in the next few weeks. With no human guide, only my guidebook, I wander the deserted muddy hillside among the broken columns and olive trees. What I am seeing is quite a mystery, at the same time most impressive. Just trying to picture what life was like when this was a thriving city almost two thousand years ago is a challenge. The most striking structure is the amphitheatre, with its nineteen tiers, renovated and used for a festival of classical drama each summer. Otherwise, in many cases there are only columns remaining, and plenty of headless statues. Most of the mosaics and statuary have been moved to the Bardo Museum in *Tunis*. As I stand on the stage looking out over the vast expanse, a couple of school groups appear in the distance. Otherwise, I have *Dougga* all to myself.

My free-lance taxi driver arrives on schedule to return me the short distance to *Dougga Nouvelle,* but none of the *louages* heading back to *Tunis* stop for me. As I wait, I watch laundry flapping in a cold wind on the flat rooftops of the village houses, and hear the *muezzin's* call to prayer, plaintive and powerful. A weathered older man keeps me company and escorts me onto the public bus, modern and very comfortable, when it finally comes. I figure this entire day of adventure has cost me a scant twenty dollars.

My black boots are caked with *Dougga* mud, but I've seen many shoeshine men on the *Tunis* streets. They patiently wait along the busy sidewalks for passing customers. Next morning I lean against a convenient tree just like a Tunisian, holding out one foot after the other until my boots are polished up like new. All for a few cents including tip.

After these few solo days, it's time to move a block or two away to the Hana International Hotel, which is upscale compared to the Carlton. I can just glimpse the sparkling blue of the bay from my seventh floor room. The Hana is bustling with tour groups, including mine. After meeting each other at dinner, my fellow travelers and I all start out the next morning by walking through a high gate to the old city, the walled *medina*, which I have merely sampled. Sunday is a good day to go there, less thronged than normal. Some 300,000 people live within its walls, one third of the population of *Tunis*. Who knows how many stalls and shops abound among the narrow winding lanes? In the days when the *medinas* first sprang up, these labyrinthine alleys were a simple defense from invasions by warring tribes, who would get trapped inside. Left to myself, I too would probably get lost here.

Our tour group of twenty-three is indeed cosmopolitan, I being the only American. The other English-speakers are two Australian women and a young Dutch couple who have lived in the States. There are four young Italians who keep to themselves, eight Argentineans—two of them lady doctors— one woman from Martinique and several French people, including three children. But the prize participant is our Tunisian guide, tall unflappable Mr. Driss. He is quite unfazed by the language requirements of our group, switching smoothly from French to Spanish to English to Italian. Arabic is his native tongue, of course. And it isn't only when he gives his tourist spiel that he is so fluent. Chatting casually with any of us, he speaks colloquially in our own lingo, virtually unaccented, and even exhibits the body language to match.

So now our bags are loaded into a van and we're on our way. The Bardo Museum in *Tunis* is home to the largest collection of Roman mosaics and statuary in the world. Artwork from many other periods is also displayed: Phoenician, Punic, Turkish, etc. Today seems to be school museum-visit day, as the place is thronged with kids of all ages and their teachers. Among all the relics on display, this human element is welcome. An optimistic camel handler waits patiently outside the Bardo beside his scrawny beast adorned in a bright saddle blanket. Will a tourist want a ride?

En route to nearby *Carthage* we drive past 2nd century Roman aqueducts, also the Café Roosevelt. (What's the story behind that name?) Although *Carthage* was once second only to *Rome* in size within the Empire, it is now virtually deserted. The museum is in a lovely setting next to the Cathedral of St. Louis, built on the site of a pagan temple. Our final stop of the day is at the picturesque village of *Sidi bou Said*, full of blinding white homes with brilliant blue doorways and shutters. If this were not the Sunday holiday, would *Sidi* be so full of visitors, mostly Tunisian, lounging at the sidewalk cafes?

This country was once considered the bread basket of *Rome*, but it is primarily olive orchards and flowering almonds that we see as we drive south on an excellent highway to the most holy city of Tunisia, *Kairouan*, which means caravan. The Great Mosque here is the oldest in North Africa. At *El Jem* is a giant coliseum which, now restored, seats thirty thousand, nearly as large as the one in *Rome*. When it was built in 235 AD, this was a crossroads for trade, but that's hard to imagine now. The building stone had to come from eighteen miles away, the water almost ten miles. What a task, to build such a behemoth in such an isolated place. I'll bet the annual music festival held here nowadays is spectacular.

After passing through industrial *Sfax* and the spice center of *Gabes*, we take a ferry across to the island of *Jerba* to spend a couple of nights. Our hotel is elegant enough to be a museum. This is the island where Ulysses and his men were supposedly detained on their return from *Troy*. The garish blue-tiled El-Ghriba synagogue here is notable for its history if not for its beauty. Dating back to 586 BC, this Jewish community is one of the oldest in the world and over the years has received many influxes of Jews fleeing persecution in Spain, Italy and Palestine.

Upon leaving the upscale island of *Jerba*, we pass through the small town of *Mareth* and make an impromptu stop at the weekly *souk*—-market. I could have bought a rabbit or a live sheep there, or plastic buckets made in India, as well as blue jeans or kitchen utensils from China, Japan, or Turkey.

Of all our Tunisian destinations, *Matmata* is surely the most fascinating for its troglodyte—underground—dwellings. For more than one thousand years, Berbers have resided in homes, some quite elaborate, dug out of the hillsides. Of the seven to eight thousand caves still existing, some are two hundred feet deep, although heavy flooding in 1969 drove many people to build what is now *New Matmata* above ground. A young woman in a wine-colored *jellabah*— caftan— sits on a mat grinding corn with a mortar and pestle at the cave which we visit. She explains that it is home for twelve people and a cat, and is built on two levels around a large open courtyard. The living room looks quite comfy but I don't think I would enjoy climbing a rickety ladder to the upper level bedrooms. Adventurous tourists can spend a night in some of these cave dwellings. I've heard the word troglodyte as long as I can remember but only now understand its true meaning.

Now we have reached the town of *Douz* and are climbing onto our handsome camels for a placid ride. The camel makes it easy for me by folding his legs and sitting down while I throw one leg over the blanket—no saddle—and settle myself on his back. Hang on though when he rises up to full height. We're led by fierce-looking turbaned tribesmen on a short circuit into the Sahara. Up high like this you get a great panoramic view of the desert, but I don't feel much like Lawrence of Arabia. Camels not only have bad tempers and often foam at the mouth, but I discover that they make obscene abdominal noises like a giant toilet being flushed. I'm in hysterics before our ride is finished.

Try to imagine seeing Antarctica in Tunisia. We're driving west across the endless white expanse of huge Chott-el-Jerid, a two million-year-old salt lake. But is that a mirage of palm trees in the distance? No, it's an oasis town near the Algerian border where we stop and wander among the groves and peer down into a deep gorge which looks like a miniature Grand Canyon. Although there are souvenir items for sale here and at most of our stops—jewelry, pottery, toy leather camels—vendors appear very casual, not at all pushy, as I had anticipated.

"There's polygamy in the palmeraie," says Driss. We're in *Tozeur*, taking a *caleche*—carriage—ride through the peaceful palm grove when he explains that it takes only one male palm tree to keep ten female trees producing.

Our return route northward on this long final day leads past arid phosphate mining country. High cactus plants form hedges which separate tobacco and other agricultural fields. At a site of more modern history, *Kasserine* is where the Allies stopped the German advance in WW II, turning the tide effectively. A bleak cold wind convinces me that Driss is not exaggerating when he tells us it sometimes snows in this bleak area.

During these eight very full days we have traveled a big loop of twelve hundred miles. *Tunis*, a welcome sight, seems very citified and civilized when we return. Here there are parking meters and streetcars and female traffic cops. Movie theatres are showing "Postman," "English Patient," and "Eyes Wide Shut." Such are the contrasts within this smallest of the North African countries.

It's time to say farewell to my tour buddies. We can relax a bit before departure, but not so the hard-working Driss. As I leave for the airport the next morning, there he is, escorting a new group of tourists heading for the *medina* to start their tour, just as we did so very recently.

Checking in for my thousand mile flight across Algeria to *Casablanca,* I'm delighted that Royal Air Maroc does not charge me for my overweight baggage. It's time to shift mental gears in preparation for Morocco, my next Mediterranean destination. Those carpet squares and I still have some far traveling to do before getting home to Florida.

BOLIVIA Salt flats

CHAPTER 9

2002
BOLIVIAN BUSES AND BLOCKADES

My heart is pumping, both from excitement at arriving on this new continent and from the altitude. *La Paz*, capital of Bolivia, is 13,000 feet high, a sharp contrast to Costa Rica, where I just finished working for a month. When I was in *Lhasa* a few years ago, the altitude of almost 12,000 feet gave me headaches, so I've brought along a supply of Diamox.

It's late and dark when my TACA flight reaches *La Paz*. Since my bag is the last one off, I have to arrange for a taxi into town alone, for five dollars. That is, I think I'll be alone, but the large man in a white sweater who is driving, allows two friends to crowd into the front seat. I have momentary doubts as to whether these three men will indeed take me to the Residencia Rosario or dump me at the side of the road. Not only do they deliver me safely, they regale me with a lengthy history lesson of Bolivia en route. I'm happy to pay an extra dollar and see them depart when I reach the hotel.

I'm on a GAP tour — Great Adventure People — with nine others, all considerably younger than I. We are from many countries — Denmark, Holland, England — and I like that.

They're well-traveled and fun to be with, even though I don't stay up as late at night as they generally do. Keltie is a young Canadian Foreign Service officer stationed in *New York City*. Frank, an inveterate world traveler, is from Holland; nothing fazes him.

During free time on our first day, Cynthia and Karen and I take a tour of the one hundred and fifty-year old San Pedro Jail, famous for being run by the inmates. Police check us in but then stay outside. Our self-appointed guide, a cocky, smooth-talking young prisoner named Luiz, who says he's from *Fairfax, VA*, is the elected mayor of the twenty-five hundred people living here, he tells us. I wish I knew more about the jail residents I observe, including women and children. The young kids can study here but before long they go "outside" to regular schools.

We are led through a maze of vending stalls, restaurants, a laundry, and a beautiful historic church, all within the prison walls. There are five different levels of housing. If the prisoner can pay for it, he stays in the five-star section where there is a Jacuzzi, even a sushi bar. This fully developed city within a city even has its own web page and radio station, we are told. Everywhere he takes us, Luiz is escorted by a burly fellow inmate named Jesus, his "bodyguard." One wonders just how open those elections were that led to his "mayorship." Three other young tourists remain behind after we've finished the tour, probably to buy drugs. It's a surrealistic situation which only begins to make sense when Luiz says "the police are even more corrupt than we are." This bizarre experience costs us each twelve dollars.

It is with some relief that we fly the next day to *Sucre*, where the altitude is only about 9,000 feet. It is the judicial capital of Bolivia while *La Paz* is the de facto capital. This charming city, a UNESCO World Heritage Site, is surrounded by snow-covered peaks. University students swarm the lovely central plaza as I sit enjoying an ice cream cone from a vendor. One of our group, young Else from Denmark, raves that she would stay here forever if she could find a way to make a living. I can relate to that. It's breathtaking—in more ways than one—to take a half-hour walk up hilly streets to the lovely whitewashed Recoleta Convent, with its view overlooking *Sucre*. Nearby is the Textile Museum, which has demonstrations of weaving as well as galleries and a shop. Churches abound, some European looking and ornate, others simple and gleaming white, like California missions.

I'm no archaeologist, but am fascinated to ride to a dusty area outside *Sucre* where there are thousands of dinosaur tracks, three and four-toed, from the late Cretacean period. They tilt up a stone hillside, originally flat, which has been raised by geologic upheavals over some eighty million years. Supposedly there are over five thousand separate footprints from dozens of different species. This site was only discovered inadvertently when a cement company started mining limestone recently.

One of the features of GAP tours is the use of public transport. So here we are on a public bus crowded among many Bolivians headed for *Potosi*, the highest city of its size in the world. On each side are cornfields, goats, donkeys and sheep under eucalyptus trees, while the road climbs and climbs some more, leaving *Sucre* far behind. An occasional TV dish rises from the roof of one of the earthen farmhouses. At every brief stop, vendors swarm aboard, selling snacks— buns or boiled potatoes. Although it's a gray day, the sharp mountain vistas are eye-catchingly beautiful. Look! An extended rainbow emerges from the clouds just as a rainbow song blares from the radio.

Finally, incongruously, we cross some railroad tracks, and a landing strip suddenly appears at our right, followed by a sign saying "Bienvenido Potosi." Why have we come here anyway? Primarily we want to explore Cerro Rico—Rich Hill—the silver mine with such incredible wealth that it enriched Spain for centuries. In fact, at the height of the 1600s silver frenzy, *Potosi* was as large a city as the *London* of those days.

For touring the mine, Wilson, our local guide, decks us out in boots, yellow slickers and hard hats. We buy cigarettes, coca leaves and dynamite as gifts for the miners. Just imagine, they have to provide their own dynamite to do their work. Carrying gas lanterns, we enter the mine, but first we must pay ritualistic homage to the statue of *El Tio*, who rules the underground. We're given a tiny cup of ninety-eight proof alcohol from which we sprinkle a few drops to "honor the earth" before knocking the rest back. Ugh. Is it that, or the low narrow tunnels and fetid air that make me decidedly queasy? Karen and Cindy and I split early, to drink in the delicious bright air outside.

No wonder the miners during their twelve-hour days need to chew plenty of coca leaves to help alleviate the depressing conditions. If a miner is lucky, he can make a hundred and fifty dollars a week. One miner we meet has worked here over thirty years, ever since he was nineteen, and proudly tells us that three of his five children are at the university in *Sucre*. Cerro Rico has been called "the mouth of Hell."

The next day we leave the Jerusalem Hotel and *Potosi* for another long bus ride to *Uyuni*. This "ghost town," as our guide calls it, is the jumping-off point for a four-day excursion on the Salar, the largest salt flats in the world and the highest. Loaded into four-wheel drive vehicles with our gear and food supplies, we're part of a small convoy crossing this seven hundred and fifty square mile area. The first day is totally surrealistic as we drive slowly through an endless shallow salt lake on invisible tracks. Surely we must be on a boat, not in a jeep. Splashing sounds reinforce the sensation. Is anyone feeling seasick? Up ahead, the bluish white water can hardly be separated from the sky, except for the perfect reflection of the clouds mirrored in the lake.

Our long day in these numbing surroundings is broken only by a lunch stop at dramatic Inkawassi — Fish Island — which is covered with a veritable forest of straight tall cactus, said to be some eight hundred years old. The only structure here, a motel made completely of salt, is no longer in use. Apparently it was built to lure tourists for the unusual experience of staying overnight in a salt hostel, but was soon closed by the government for environmental reasons. (I speculate that that means lack of plumbing.) Late that afternoon we suddenly find ourselves on dry land and on an actual track at that. How on earth do the drivers know where to leave the shimmering lake when there is no visible roadway?

The next few days we drive through bleak brown plains, surrounded by a ring of low mountains and volcanoes, mostly snow-covered, known as the "Ring of Fire." Weird eroded rock formations of the Western Cordilleras remind me of our western United States, except for an occasional lake full of showy stinky flamingos. More than once, a vehicle in our little procession gets stuck in the mud. When that happens to us, I can't get out of the van without sinking into ankle deep muck. Roberto, our driver, and the others hook up chain and tackle with the efficiency of long practice and slowly winch us free. Gradually we reach farmland populated by llamas and planted with quinoa, the nutritious Andean grain that is a staple of this area. The llamas wear bright yarn tassels in their ears at this season. I don't understand the reason but it makes for great photos. By the time we return to *Uyuni* on our fourth day, that "ghost town" looks downright civilized, and hot showers feel mighty good.

That evening we board a big overnight public bus — the last leg of this trip — for a twelve-hour ride on a primary well-traveled road north to *La Paz*. Except for one half-hour rest stop and a couple of emergency pit stops, riding through the night on this bumpy road is soporific despite the cold.

Suddenly, about four-thirty a.m. I wake up, realizing we have come to a dead halt behind two large trucks full of squealing pigs. Nothing is moving ahead of us or behind, but we hear gunfire in the distance. We mutter and grumble, speculating as to what is causing the delay.

When it gets light enough, I venture out to stretch my legs and check things out. While squatting behind scrubby bushes up on the hillside, I count fifty-nine large vehicles immobilized by what turns out to be a tin miners' road blockade. Rumors of violence abound. What to do? We have only minimal snacks for food and feel anxious as well as hungry. Jon, our GAP tour leader, spells out the limited options and after taking a vote, our little band decides to walk past the blockade. It's now nine-thirty. We don't want to wait till later in the day when the strikers might well get drunk and unpredictable. We drag our luggage down from the top of the bus and start off. Keltie kindly stashes my small pack atop her wheeled bag, so I have it easy.

Needless to say, I refrain from taking pictures of the strikers as we trudge along what seems a great distance but is really only two miles. The men are lounging by the left roadside; we keep our eyes averted and stick to the right side. Once safely beyond them, we find taxis which have brought the wives there to deliver food and drink for the miners. Our group happily piles into taxis to go to the next town, *Oruro*. At the bus station there we're delighted to find a proper bathroom—with hair dryers yet—and we buy soft drinks, but still no hot food. Luckily the twelve-thirty bus has enough seats for us. Instead of reaching *La Paz* at seven a.m. it is five-thirty p.m. when we walk through the welcoming doors of the Residencia Rosario, weary but grateful to have arrived safely.

Strangely enough, except for mild headaches and sleeplessness, my only real problem with Bolivia's altitude comes when we get back to *La Paz*. Here, on our final morning I have two severe nosebleeds. Fortunately, my roommate

Cindy, a teacher from New Hampshire, is there to give me a hand. Except for wandering the so-called Witches' Market near by, I take it easy all day. We've all been drinking lots of coca tea, which is found in most of the hotel lobbies, or chewing coca leaves. They're dry and tasteless, a little like bay leaves, but serve to counteract the effects of altitude. No, they're not narcotic—not till they've been processed into cocaine.

The next day I leave the "Tibet of the Alps" for Peru. And oh yes, we discovered that the reason for the miners' blockade had nothing to do with pay or working conditions. Instead, it was a protest to the government for having appointed a *woman* to be the head of their company.

PERU Trading on the Amazon

CHAPTER 10

2002
PIRANHA FOR DINNER?

It's six-thirty and just getting dark as our launch pulls away from our ship, the Rio Amazonas, to explore some small tributaries of the mighty Amazon. The jungle seems to enclose us while we silently drift along. Alfredo's strong flashlight keeps roaming through the dense vegetation in search of wildlife. Oh yes, there's an owl butterfly, looking for all the world like a miniature owl, not much bigger than my thumbnail. A shrill chorus of tree frogs serenades us. And then, look up! Through the overhanging branches, the night sky is brilliant with stars, the Southern Cross clearly defined. A magical moment.

My *Sarasota* friend, Orv, and I are cruising on the Upper Amazon for one week in early March. Much to our delight, there are only two other passengers—and sixteen crew— aboard this sturdy comfortable 146-foot long vessel when we leave *Iquitos*, Peru. At this point, two thousand miles from its mouth in Brazil, the Amazon is one mile wide and deep enough for ocean-going ships. Although I think I could have chugged along this great river happily for many days without making landfall or feeling bored, we're offered an active schedule of shore excursions, early and late, two to four times daily, led by the almost too-knowledgeable Alfredo.

One of our first stops is at a rum "factory," if you can dignify this operation with that word. Sugar cane is being processed in a very rustic barn with primitive equipment. At the invitation of the handsome owner, Cesar, we climb up to visit his large stilt house. Relaxing in a breezy open-sided room, we are served thimble-sized samples of flavored rum. Guess what? We end up buying pint bottles of ginger and other exotically flavored rums. Served with a coke every day at Happy Hour aboard ship, they are a tasty investment.

Twice we stop at Indian villages where we are escorted to a ceremonial round house to view traditional dances. Although normal attire here is Western, both men and women dancers wear simple garments made from the bark of a jungle tree—*llanchama*—painted with native designs. The *Yagua* Indian dresses look a little like flour sacks, but in the *Bora* village the women go topless; their necklaces of feathers and natural seed pods substitute for blouses. I must say, the dancers of all ages seem to be enjoying themselves, smiling and laughing as they dance in a big circle to the beat of "talking drums." Good sport Orv jumps up to join their dance while I take pictures.

Afterward we wander around the large communal room, chatting with the women and viewing the array of handicrafts which are for sale or barter. Bark paintings, gourd rattles, carved statues and masks, necklaces—everything is made with natural materials from the jungle. In exchange, instead of cash, we trade school supplies—such as crayons or felt markers—or combs and makeup. We've been forewarned and have brought along trading items. Orv's bright cotton bandana is much admired; she trades it for a wild necklace of feathers and dried seedpods. Everybody is happy.

I had rather assumed the insects would be bad on the river, but when we're under way, they are no problem. Ashore for a jungle walk, though, no amount of insect repellent guarantees us protection from the swarms of hungry mosquitoes. I invariably come back sticky, hot, and covered with bites. In the forest it is always dark, the dense tree canopy is far overhead, and the air is stifling. We step carefully along the spongy boggy jungle trails. Alfredo warns us to keep a wary eye out for anaconda snakes, but that may just be Alfredo acting the know-it-all leader. Anyway, nobody sees any snakes at all, but we do see busy trails of indomitable fire ants, just like in any Florida yard.

Some hanging vines are long and strong enough to swing from. One of our group plays at being Tarzan, not I. There are giant ficus trees, tiny wild orchids hiding among the vines, and an occasional splash of bright foliage—*heliconia*. Trudging silently in single file behind Alfredo, we hear plenty of jungle sounds but see no monkeys and only an occasional bird. A sweet putrid aroma suffuses the heavy air, somewhere between perfume and reeking garbage. I can't wait to breathe fresh air again.

Back on the launch, we have one grand sighting of a three-toed sloth making its slow way down a tree trunk, too distant to get a clear photograph. Where a narrow stream unexpectedly widens into a swampy lake one day, we find ourselves surrounded by giant water lily pads—*Victoria Regia*—and their variegated blooms, white one day, changing to pink the next, and gone the next. From the deck of the Amazonas one can sometimes spot dolphins, usually gray, but once I see a solitary pink dolphin which is specific to this river and highly endangered. These friendly mammals are said to have a brain capacity forty percent larger than that of humans.

After three days and some three hundred and twenty-five miles, we dock one morning at *Santa Rosa*, the easternmost Peruvian point on the Amazon. This is known as *Tres Fronteras*. With a day mostly free to explore, we seize the opportunity to visit the border town of *Leticia*, Colombia. Tempted by its proximity, we then take a short taxi ride into the equally unimpressive town of *Tabatinga* in Brazil. Not only have I never been to either of these countries before, I don't recall ever having visited three separate countries in such a short space of time. No customs formalities are required either. We check out the markets, disappointingly ordinary, with no exotic produce to remind us of where we are. To commemorate this three-pronged frontier, we drink a beer together with Jorge, our taxi driver, in Colombia, in Brazil, and then in Peru, all in the course of two and a half hours.

Back on the Amazonas by mid-afternoon, we snooze a bit while waiting for new passengers to arrive. The first pair headed back to *Iquitos* by fast launch early this morning. Now two new couples are joining us for the upriver half of the voyage. No sooner do they climb aboard than a fierce squall erupts, with lightning and sheeting rain, actually whipping up whitecaps. The ship remains under-populated, but Alfredo is rejuvenated to have new victims for his encyclopedic monologues. These sudden storms are common, although only once do we get drenched while wandering through a riverside village.

The hundred-year-old Scottish-built Rio Amazonas is mostly air conditioned, with handsome dark paneling in the dining room lounge. Cabins are small, but since Orv and I have been given separate rooms, it's no problem. There's no hot water, nor do we really need it. Tap water is the color of tea, but we still manage to do hand laundry in it. The crew couldn't be nicer, although they can't be making much money off so few of us. The excellent menu includes such local standards as plantain, yucca and fresh hearts of palm. We eat plenty of fish, including what we've caught on fishing expeditions—catfish and piranha. Whoever knew that that deadly fish was edible? The catfish is far tastier, if you ask me, and has fewer bones.

Our favorites among the crew are Ulderico, a 41-year old Jack-of-all-trades who has his eye on blonde Orv. Steady and adaptable, he is often in charge up in the wheelhouse and always pilots the launch when we explore the bayous and tributaries. Charming young moon-eyed Lider is our room steward, who sometimes appears up on deck in the evening, ostensibly to practice his English with me. Much as we enjoy their attention, Orv and I wonder if both of these Peruvian boatmen are angling for an invitation to visit the United States.

I had expected the jungle to blanket both banks of the broad brown river, but the reality is more varied. Some areas are distinctly rural, with farm animals visible, and sugar cane or other cultivated fields stretching away from the river. Houses are typically built on stilts as protection from flooding. The low banks are eroding away, and I even watch one day as a tree is uprooted by the pull of the river until it falls into the water and totally vanishes. I can hardly believe my eyes. Although floodwaters nourish the forest and land, the river is growing ever wider, eating away at subsistence farms day after day.

Everywhere we land we are immediately surrounded by children. But they don't beg, as in many poor parts of the world. They smile and chatter and follow us around till we feel like Pied Pipers. We must seem like creatures from another world, a welcome diversion in their routine lives. The murky river is used for everything by the villagers—washing clothes, shampooing hair, and of course transportation. Dugout canoes are everywhere. Without roads, they provide the only means of getting to the next farm or to school, and of course are used for fishing. Catfish are a staple of the diet.

Life along the Amazon has changed little for centuries. Some lucky villages now have electricity for a few hours daily. There are reputedly one hundred and thirty different tribes throughout Peru, of which a few still use the blowgun for hunting. I find it hard to imagine daily life in these remote settlements, without even the basic trappings of civilization which we believe necessary.

One of our final shore excursions is to visit a leprosarium in *San Pablo*, run by French nuns. Clean and spacious, it has only a few patients now, unlike when Che Guevara spent a life-changing few weeks there in 1952, an episode depicted in the popular film, "Motorcycle Diaries."

Our week passes all too quickly. We've become quite accustomed to the slow pace and muted sounds of river life by the time we disembark from the Rio Amazonas in *Iquitos.* The hustle of that small city is disconcerting now, although it had seemed quite sleepy when we first arrived there from *Lima*. *Iquitos*, population four hundred thousand, is the largest city in the Peruvian Amazon, yet can be reached only by air or river—or on foot. The city bustles with small three-wheeled *motokars*—what would be called *tuk-tuks* in Southeast Asia. It is said to be the largest city in the world with no road connecting it to the rest of the country.

We're headed next to *Lima* to start a *Machu Picchu* excursion. In the airport waiting room is a large colorful mural showing monkeys and macaws and an anaconda, beside a beautiful blue river. Although we saw none of those things—certainly not a *blue* Amazon—we did see a fascinating part of the world, and we liked what we saw. Suppose Ulderico and Lider will turn up on our doorsteps here in Florida some day?

AUSTRALIA Pelican Lagoon

CHAPTER 11

2003
STALKING THE SHY ECHIDNA
or How I Got All Scratched Up on Kangaroo Island

It's seven in the morning and I'm trying to blow the conch shell to awaken my fellow Earthwatch volunteers on *Kangaroo Island*. My efforts a dismal failure, I hike through the trees to our tents and huts banging on a kitchen basin instead. It's another day of radio tracking echidnas and goannas under Peggy Rismiller's guidance, and we're all hopeful of finding a new critter to add to those already being monitored.

This hundred-acre private nature preserve, Pelican Lagoon, is on the eastern end of *Kangaroo Island*, which floats just a few miles south of South Australia. My five teammates and I flew the short distance from *Adelaide* on Emu Air. And I thought the emu was a bird that couldn't fly. One also could have come by ferryboat. It's February, summertime in these southern latitudes.

Approaching on a very rutty road, I'm quite unimpressed with the grounds and buildings where we'll be staying for two weeks. Except for the attractive lodge which serves as dining hall, lounge and lab, all the buildings at the Pelican

Lagoon Research Center have been built from salvaged materials by Mike, Peggy's partner. They may not be very beautiful but they're all environmentally sound. Jean and Kazuko and I share a decidedly rustic cabin through which the wind whistles. Thank goodness it's not wintertime. Plastic sheeting substitutes for windows around three sides of our large single room. It makes a great racket in the wind but doesn't drown out the sound of the possums playing on the tin roof at night.

Whole families of kangaroos, nurtured over the years by Peggy and Mike, hang out around the grounds, nibbling choice vegetation and awaiting kitchen handouts. Ruby Roo and her grandchildren, Mover and Shaker, usually greet us when we walk to the lodge for breakfast. I've never been panhandled by kangaroos before.

What exactly are we here for anyway? Well, in the last fifteen years, ninety spiny echidnas have been identified on this research preserve. Perhaps twenty echidnas and a dozen goannas are on our current roster of animals, having been given names and a radio chip, and then released. We volunteers usually head out in pairs, equipped with radio tracking equipment and compasses and maps, in hopes of finding specific animals that are expected to lay their eggs at this time of year. We are supposed to observe many things around us, most importantly the numerous chest-high termite mounds in which the goannas dig a burrow and carefully deposit their eggs. Every bit of the information we gather goes into Peggy's data bank.

What, you might ask, is the point of all this detailed research. Well, little is known about the echidna, which looks very much like our porcupine but is totally unrelated. An echidna weighs between five and ten pounds. Considering that it has existed for an amazing 110 million years, it must be doing something right. Maybe it has some useful secrets to teach us. Peggy, although an American scientist, is the recognized authority on Australian echidnas, and is invited to participate and present at many international symposia. She created this protected enclave fifteen years ago.

The echidna and the platypus are the only two creatures belonging to a category known as monotremes—egg laying mammals. In fact, the echidna is the most widespread native Australian mammal, and Australia is the only place this particular echidna is found. Its single egg is carried in its pouch; the young is known as a *puggle*. Isn't that a wonderful name? It is a shy creature, with its golden brown spines providing excellent camouflage, and is able to vanish in a flash by burrowing down into leaf litter at the foot of a tree. Its only natural predator here is the goanna, about which we are also collecting data. In other parts of the world they are known as monitor lizards.

After our first day of orientation, I note in my journal, "steep learning curve here." We're given different assignments each day after breakfast, and once we pick up the signal from our assigned animal, we are supposed to follow it no matter where it leads us. If a goanna is out sunning itself on a rock, that is easy. We simply record the location, the specific vegetation in that area and other details.

Unfortunately, those conditions never seem to happen for me. It isn't for lack of trying. The terrain is hilly, either woodland or grassland or shrubland. Even with a compass I manage to get lost, or lose the radio signal or spend hours wandering around. Pelican Lagoon preserve is rather like a peninsula, so just when I think a glimpse of water will help orient me, I realize that there's water on other sides, too. Many times I plunge valiantly into a dense thicket of prickly acacia, shoulder high, holding my unwieldy telemetry device aloft, intent on the signal which leads me onward, but my sightings are few. Prickly acacia is well-named. I often bring home prickers imbedded in my arms and legs. Despite the midday heat, we have good reason to wear jeans and long-sleeved shirts for protection.

I certainly don't need to take my usual early morning walk, as I've done for many years whether at home or abroad. Here we cover many miles in the course of each long day, intent on landmarks and the beeps of our radio tracking devices. Jean, from Oregon, is our star volunteer and even finds and brings in a new echidna that hasn't been logged in yet. Whoever discovers a new echidna has the privilege of giving it a name; this one becomes Jebe. Among the other long-time echidnas we're monitoring are Sommer and Solstice. Two of our goannas are named Charlie and Slinkie, both females about ready to lay eggs.

Among the other volunteers on our team are petite Kazuko from *Tokyo* and enthusiastic Becky from *Melbourne*, Australia, who works for Shell Oil. She received a scholarship from them to participate in this Earthwatch expedition. Our only male volunteer is nineteen-year old Chris, who is on a gap year between high school graduation and entering college next year. He worked on Wall Street for some months before coming to *Kangaroo Island*. After this he's heading to New Zealand for an Earthwatch project about dolphins, following which he'll fly to Panama and sail with family members to the *Galapagos Islands*. Wow! College may seem tame after such a vagabond year.

Although my teammates have better success over our two weeks, I do have some close contact with the captured critters when they're brought in for lab testing. Jett is the first echidna that I see up close. I help take temperatures and other measurements for our database. One wouldn't want to "pet" these critters, because their spines—not actual quills, although the difference is unclear to me—are indeed sharp. But with Peggy holding him firmly, he's shy and docile, so that you can stroke downward over his mottled coat of hard golden spines. When we're finished with him, he seems happy to be released out in the same wooded area where he was captured, and quickly vanishes.

My last couple of days I offer to be more productive by entering tracking records into Peggy's computer. At least I can't get lost doing that. And it's cozy to work in her office trailer hidden in the woods while the others are braving a cold rainy drizzle outside. When it rains, big black biting ants appear and swarm up your pants leg before you know it, but not where I work.

A village woman named Coral cooks for us our first few days, but now we volunteers are doing kitchen duty one day each week. Since we're nowhere near a town or grocery store, the storeroom and freezer are kept well stocked. Breakfasts and lunches are casual, do-it-yourself style, but each volunteer chef tries to vary the rather mundane cuisine by producing an interesting menu for the evening meal, with mixed results. Kazuko's teriyaki dinner is a hit, as are the banana splits we have for dessert one evening. I of course make a soup of leftovers, and Chris bakes chocolate chip cookies from scratch one night, to our delight. We taste an Australian pancake called a *pikelet*. It's a pleasant break to pore over Peggy's library of cookbooks in the unusual quiet of the lodge, while the others are all out on their scavenger hunts.

Cleaning up is also a shared assignment, with careful attention to the perpetual water shortage. Solar panels provide hot water. The bright eyes of a possum at the kitchen window remind us to share the garbage with the animals waiting outside for a handout.

And then there are the solar showers. Although it's quite cool in the evenings, the days get hot, but we take showers only every second day or so because doing so is so arduous. On shower days, before reporting for duty in the morning, we fill heavy black vinyl solar bags with five gallons of water from a hose, and leave them out on the rocks all day for the sun to heat them up. Late in the afternoon we take turns, depending on how dire our need is for a shower. It's a cooperative effort. You get a partner to help you lift up the heavy bag of—hopefully—hot water and dump it into a huge bucket which sits on a high tree stump outside the shower hut. Then both of you tug and strain to hoist the bucket up as high as you can, tying the rope tight to keep it suspended. Tubing from the bucket leads into a breezy little corrugated hut where gravity directs the water through a showerhead. When you're hot and sticky and tired enough, this refreshes you almost as much as a "real" shower.

Not our whole time is spent working. On two different days, big burly Mike drives us to rocky beaches where we watch great numbers of sea lions cavorting around. We can see clearly across the fifteen miles to the southern Australian coast. Then it's a visit to a eucalyptus distillery, and into *Kingscote* to watch the pelicans at feeding time. That evening we join a local family for a dinner of fish and chips, topped off with the fabulous Australian dessert, *pavlova*. Another time we view the small fairy penguins near *Penneshaw*, the only other town on this island, and stop for ice cream afterward.

Kangaroo Island, ninety-three miles long and only thirty-three miles wide, has about four thousand residents but is beginning to attract retirees and tourists. It is a scenic laid-back place. I sure hope it doesn't lose its charm by becoming "touristy." Short-term visitors would certainly enjoy the beaches and lovely countryside, but I doubt they would have the fun that we did learning about those intriguing goannas and echidnas at Pelican Lagoon. Or leave with as many scratches as I did.

NAMIBIA Chewbaaka in his play tree

CHAPTER 12

2004
UP CLOSE WITH THE CHEETAH

Have you ever rested your hands willingly on a cheetah? Through Earthwatch assignments I've had close contact with Indian wolves, Mediterranean dolphins and Australian echidnas. Now I'm in the southern African country of Namibia to work with that elegant endangered cat, the cheetah.

Little did I know, however, that we would have *such* close contact. The first of my two weeks here, our resident cheetahs are being captured, five each day, and brought to our clinic for their annual physical exams. I'm glad it isn't I who has to dart the animal with anesthetic, although I'm very brave at handling the *sleeping* cat and even taking its pulse and rectal temperature.

Dr. Arthur Bagot-Smith, the vet, has flown in in his private plane from the nearby town of *Otjiwarongo* to conduct workups during this whole week. Several minor surgeries are required to repair surface wounds on the animals' legs. We're assigned to help Audrey, the resident vet's assistant, and to keep close records. When each cat is carried to the recovery room we take turns monitoring it, hoping it will wake up with no ill effects from the anesthetic.

The Cheetah Conservation Fund, founded by American Dr. Laurie Marker in 1990, has been instrumental in rescuing many wounded cheetahs and in educating the local cattle ranchers in better management tactics. Traditionally, the cheetah was perceived to be the enemy, just as the wolf has long been viewed by western farmers in our country. Laurie travels the world telling the story of this ancient animal, which has existed for 200,000 years and was revered by the Egyptians. I am amazed to learn that two species of cheetah once roamed North America. Now there are 12,000 to 15,000 of them in various African countries, the largest number of them here in Namibia. Her dedication is paying off.

Bonnie Schumann is the voice of CCF among Namibia's German and Afrikaans farmers, encouraging them to call us whenever a cheetah is found on their property. These are huge spreads which have been owned more often than not by the same family for generations. Some ranchers are stubborn; some more enlightened. Bonnie and her twin sister Mandy, from South Africa, are called research assistants but in fact they manage the day-to-day operations at CCF, since Laurie is away so much. Bonnie always wears a dark green shirt, Mandy wears aqua, the only way we can tell these twins apart.

Although we Earthwatch volunteers aren't directly involved, the farm also breeds Anatolian guard dogs. These robust tawny beauties are trained to safely protect farmers' livestock from wild cheetahs. Any area rancher who promises to follow prescribed safe management policies is *given* one of these valuable, highly intelligent watchdogs, an ingenious indirect way to minimize the number of cheetahs being shot or trapped.

The ideal, of course, is to rescue a trapped cheetah, check

its health and then release it into the wild. But each of our twenty-five resident cats has a history that precludes its being able to live independently, and so they live safely in huge expanses on CCF's five farms, which cover a total of thirty thousand acres. One may have a disabling injury, or another's mother might have been killed before the cub learned to hunt for itself.

After our first week of playing vet's assistant, we follow a more typical routine, exercising the cats, feeding them carefully weighed portions of raw donkey meat and updating the records. We drive slowly along the dusty trails within one of the enclosures while Merlot or Shiraz or another cat darts out to claim his personal meal flung from the back of the pickup. How the staff can identify and understand each one of these animals so intimately amazes me. Although a mother cheetah knows her cubs by the distinctive design of the spots, as individual as a fingerprint, to my untrained eye all of our cats look and act virtually alike.

All except nine-year old Chewbaaka, known as the CCF ambassador. Chewbaaka, whom Laurie has raised from a cub, is the tamest of all our cats, and often accompanies Laurie when she gives talks. We take him out to his favorite "play tree" one day, where he climbs up and contentedly poses for us at eye level. One by one, we approach deliciously near to him for close-up photos. I note in my journal, "He's a big baby." At our farewell party at Laurie's house, Chewbaaka is present, but stays in a bedroom. I think of him as almost a member of her family, and indeed, she says that she is the only mother he has ever known.

The nearest enclosure which we walk by daily is maybe two hundred meters square and is home to three females named Dusty, Sandi and Blondie. A couple of times a week they are exercised by enticing them to chase after a red flag moving on a low lure course around the perimeter, as you might see at dog races. It's funny to watch how they share the course and run in relays instead of competing with each other. The cheetah that snares the red cloth is rewarded with a hand-fed treat of raw meat. I'm just as glad I'm not asked to do that, but nobody working there appears to be missing a finger or hand. You might think these fastest of all land mammals would not need encouragement to stay fit, but since their food is delivered to each of them individually, they miss the normal exercise they would get from hunting their prey.

One morning we load up a newly acquired cheetah that has passed his health inspection and drive the pickup truck a couple of hours away to a friendly rancher's spread. Ralf, who has twelve hundred cattle, is amiable to our releasing this cat on his land, not the first time CCF has done so. But first, we sit around their dining table drinking coffee and eating pastries, talking with the farm couple about their lives. Ralf grew up here; Marion is from Germany. Their four children attend a German school in *Otjiwarongo*. I am moved to hear Marion relate how she has come to love this land so much that she could never imagine returning to Germany to live. We drive our van to the release site, slide open the door of the wooden cage and watch as the cheetah warily peeks out before suddenly leaping forward and racing far out of sight.

On our very first day, after the clinic has closed, Karen, an enthusiastic long-time volunteer from *San Diego*, takes us "newbies" on a game drive to a large open area called the "Little Serengeti" in the shadow of the Waterberg Plateau. Bumping along a rutted trail or out on the open range, we don't need binoculars to see herds of hartebeest, striking oryx—gray, black and white striped—comical warthogs and other wildlife. At this season many have their young with them. Marabou storks seem to be posing motionless atop almost every high termite mound. A couple of days later, up in "the Hide," an observation tower overlooking this same plain, most of the CCF staff gather at dusk for a surprise 27th birthday party for Jen, a long-time volunteer. What a way to celebrate, watching a brilliant sunset, surrounded by free range herds of wild game.

We Earthwatch volunteers are housed in *rondavels*, round clay huts in traditional African style, with peaked thatch roofs, but with the luxury of a window and even a sink in each. The first—and most vital—advice I'm given by Audrey upon arrival is never *ever* to walk barefoot, outside or even inside. The reason becomes obvious when the soles of my sandals collect innumerable sharp sand spurs from walking the short path to the shower bathroom. They're well named, *Devil's Thorns*. It is indeed a devilish job to remove them. With bare feet, chances are you'll only step on one once.

Outside, scrubby, shrubby low trees seem to be adorned with many small hanging pouches. Look closely, and pretty soon you'll see a small bird dart into one of these, which turns out to be a nest for the solitary weaver bird. Later in my travels, I'll see huge tent-like webs in camel thorn trees— nests for the sociable weaver bird's extended family. And then there are the bold hornbills here which sharpen their long beaks by tapping endlessly on the windows of the clinic or the windshields of the trucks. American woodpeckers are wimps by comparison.

Here on this five thousand foot high plateau, the weather is so nice that we usually eat outside under a flapping waterproof tarp. A staff cook prepares some of our meals, but the rest of us pitch in as well, even the resident scientists. One day I assist Amy at sautéing and stuffing a Namibian delicacy—giant mushrooms. The local name is *omajewa* and they are bigger than a round serving platter. We've seen them growing at the base of the tall termite mounds, looking for all the world like huge white flowers, maybe hormone enhanced. This is the season apparently, and we vegetarians gorge on them. A single mushroom serves several people amply. More typical meals include pasta, salads and hamburgers. Alex, a smiling young gal from Italy, makes scrumptious crepes for a Sunday morning treat.

Driving to one of the farms to feed our cheetahs, we almost always see a family of warthogs scurrying across the dusty lane ahead of us. An African wild pig, they have scrawny legs and a tail that sticks straight up like an antenna. I'm not so good at spotting game yet, but those with trained eyes often point out giraffes poised behind trees at the side of the track, their long necks mimicking the angle of the tree trunks. What a thrill, on our final feeding excursion, to see eland, three zebra and an incredible dozen or more giraffe at separate spots along the dirt road. A record, to give me lasting memories.

We've been so absorbed in CCF activities that we've hardly strayed from this central highland area outside *Otjiwarongo*, in the shadow of the stunning Waterberg Plateau. But the end of our time here draws near. It's a small caravan which loads up to drive into *Windhoek* on Sunday to deliver us volunteers to the airport or to other destinations. We even have Carrie in a crate in the back. She will have surgery tomorrow for a broken leg. That is a common condition for cheetahs, whose bones are fragile. Our cheetahs are fed a calcium supplement with their ration of raw donkey meat to counteract this genetic problem.

Transition: from a working volunteer and vet's assistant, I now transform into a safari tourist. Monday morning I join a small band of young European travelers loading up with tents and sleeping bags to take a nine-day "Chameleon" safari. Our work at CCF was active, though not strenuous. From now on I'll be more of an observer, covering a wide loop through this southwest African nation.

Namibia, long a German protectorate, still shows German influence in the picturesque church spires—Lutheran—that would look proper in Bavaria, and in the sausages and cheeses available in the supermarkets. Independence came in 1990. The capital of *Windhoek* is a charming city of only

245,000. Twice the size of California, Namibia has vast open spaces and only five people per square mile on average. Although English is the official language, Afrikaans is widely spoken, as well as the native tongues of eleven indigenous tribes, including a clicking dialect.

The Namib Desert, one of the oldest deserts in the world, runs the length of Namibia's almost thousand mile long coast. Driving southwest from *Windhoek* across the Great Sand Sea on a good highway, we're surrounded by spectacular red dunes, high in iron content, long before we see the coast. Watching the sun set over Elim's Dune reminds me of sunset at Ayers Rock in Australia, with similar ochre and brick-red vistas. I renege on climbing up the slipping sandy dune with the others, but do go to watch the sun rise from Dune 45 very early the next morning. The dimming shadows and increasing brilliance on the stark sandy shapes, minus virtually any greenery, are stunning. These so-called "star" dunes are as much as thirty miles from the sea and shift very little. Later that same day we trudge down a steep rough trail to the floor of Sesriem Canyon, a spectacular slot canyon reputedly thirty million years old.

What a contrast after a long dusty drive up the coast, to arrive at the popular seaside town of *Swakopmund*, west of *Windhoek*. Here are shops and palmy oases and a small charming museum. Continuing north, we see many sea birds and a huge colony of Cape fur seals. Watching the young seals learning to fend for themselves in the water is amusing, but the stench of the nesting area is overwhelming, and they sure are noisy.

We've been setting up our little dome tents each night at wonderfully managed campsites with clean "ablution blocks," all except at *Swakopmund* where we stay in bungalows and sleep on real beds. I don't miss the sound of jackals rooting around outside our tents at all. My assigned tent mate is a pretty German gal with the unusual name of

Silka. She's shy when speaking English with me, but skilful using her hairdresser's shears to trim my hair one day. After a few nights she moves in with one of the young German men but often gives me a hand raising my tent or packing it up in the morning.

Benny, our dusky Namibian driver/guide, has brought all the foodstuffs which we pitch in to prepare; cleanup likewise is communal. Tonight we're going to rough it at a remote bush camp, nestled at the foot of stark cliffs which appear sensuous in dawn's first light. Tomorrow we hope to seek out the elusive small desert elephants as we swing northeast toward Etosha Park. But it is not to be.

Shortly after gassing up at a town with the unlikely name of *Uis*, our van stops short behind a vehicle which has just overturned on the road ahead of us. The young blonde German driver, Eva, has been thrown through the windshield and is covered in blood. Our rescue crew barrels into action. Fortunately, Benny comes from this area and knows the nearest medical facilities. As we ply Eva with juice and water in our van and apply ice to her wounds, Benny floors it. In less than an hour we reach a small hospital at *Khorixas*, where she is admitted and ends up requiring fourteen stitches in her scalp. My fellow safari-mates are all German, so are able to reassure Eva, and eagerly buy her some supplies from the nearest convenience store. Friends will come to rescue her later.

When we finally resume our travels, it has been raining so hard that the Unib River has flooded and we're unable to ford it. So it's back to *Khorixas* for the night before taking an alternative route to *Outjo* through the next morning's rain. Instead of desert elephants, we encounter a bedraggled group of bicyclists on safari in this miserable weather. It makes us feel snug and smug in our van.

For much of this safari I sit up front with the driver, while the rest of the group chatter away at great length in German. Not only is youthful Benny able and reliable, he can answer all my questions in good English. When the news comes on the radio in the Damara or Khoi-Khoi language—with all those clicking sounds—he translates, and demonstrates the language for me, much to my amusement. Benny proves to be far better company than the young Germans.

Etosha Park is vast, full of game and minus many tourists. Once you enter the park, you can get out of your vehicle only at a few specified places, so the animals know that they're safe. That makes for great visibility of plenty of zebra, herds of springboek, wildebeest, oryx, and finally even lions and elephants. Oh yes, and flamingoes at Fischer's Pan. It's hard to take in all the varied wildlife we're seeing across the mostly barren plains on every side, all except leopard, which I keep hoping to spot but never do. Well-kept waterholes lure the animals, especially when natural water supplies are low. Altogether we stay overnight at three different sites in fabulous Etosha Park.

I had gazed often at the long red bluff of Waterberg Plateau from my CCF *rondavel*, so now it's fun to spend a night at the park there. This is the last night to pitch my little tent before our return to *Windhoek*, where I look forward to a hot shower and a couple of days rest before heading next to Swaziland. I happen to thrive on variety. This safari has given me a look at the wild beauty of Namibia and been an interesting contrast to the work at CCF. Sometimes called a stark paradise, Namibia has proven truly captivating.

GUATEMALA Mighty Tikal

CHAPTER 13

2005
MACAWS, MONKEYS AND MOLAS

Guatemala

Guatemala has sounded exotic to me ever since my childhood, when an adventurous aunt went there and brought back bright hand-woven gifts and tales of her travels. Since then I've lived and voyaged much farther afield without the slightest curiosity about Guatemala or its neighbors. But this year I've decided to roam the length of Central America, piecing together two to three-week segments in several of these small connecting countries.

For starters, three friends from *Washington DC* join me on a tour of Mayan sites primarily in Guatemala but including brief forays into Honduras and Belize. Bill, Tom, Margaret and I have known each other since our days in *Madras*, India. Despite being very well-traveled, they are as unfamiliar with this part of the world as I. Tom's ability at Spanish is a Godsend to the rest of us. Our first stop is at *Antigua*, so charming that I look forward to returning there for a week of Spanish study after this tour ends. Our elegant hotel with its lush courtyard was once the governor's mansion; when I return I'll be staying in a local home. Cobblestone streets, a central plaza complete with fountain, and partially reconstructed churches attest to its early days as the Spanish colonial capital before an earthquake leveled much of the city.

Colorful *Chichicastenango* is primarily a festive market town where we are surrounded by brightly garbed Mayan women and extensive handicraft stalls. It would be easy for me to lose myself among these vendors for days on end although I'm not much of a shopper usually. I wonder if this is where Aunty Dee bought those woven sashes so long ago.

On a ferry ride across stunning Lake Atitlan, surrounded by brisk whitecaps, Tom and I go topside where we sit on white vinyl chairs viewing the volcanoes. All of a sudden the boat lurches, Tom and his chair skitter toward the rail, and I feel sure that he's in for an unscheduled bath. But no, he hangs onto the rail while his beloved L. L. Bean hat gets caught in the wind and swept overboard. Whew! We promptly join the others safe down below, where he bemoans the loss of his hat. But when we disembark at the town of *Santiago Atitlan*, who is the first vendor awaiting us? Yes, a hat salesman. So Tom replaces his expensive fedora with a local version which stands him in good stead for the rest of our trip.

Altogether we visit six Mayan sites, the first being Copan in Honduras, memorable for the cheeky macaws which act as a welcoming committee at the entrance. Quirigua, back over the border into Guatemala, is in the center of a banana plantation. A side trip takes us to the picturesque Spanish fort of San Felipe, in the Rio Dulce area.

Several hours north, we reach the largest temple—and most powerful in its day—Tikal, situated in the heart of the Peten jungle. Our bungalows are within the national park itself so we can wander around the ruins freely at any time of day or night. Initially I feel as though I am in Africa, hearing terrifyingly loud roars. But it is not lions, only howler monkeys, whose voices sound very near while they themselves stay hidden in the foliage. Not till I'm in Nicaragua do I finally see monkeys. Tikal translates to mean "Place of Voices," but I don't think that refers to monkeys' voices.

After centuries of dominance over the other Mayan city-states, Tikal collapsed and was abandoned about 900 AD, probably from over-population. Its many buildings rapidly hidden by the voracious jungle, it was not till 1800 that it was rediscovered. Climbing steep steps up to Temple 5, we easily see why. Except for a few emerging pyramid shapes, we're surrounded by a sea of dense green forest as far as the eye can see. The next two sites, Yaxhe and Zunantunich are smaller and not so memorable.

Although Tikal is so highly touted, I personally find Caracol the most appealing. Maybe it's because we have such a long ride over such terrible roads to reach it. We're in Belize now, staying at the delightful DuPlooy's Jungle Lodge for our final few nights of the tour. If you get up early, you can sip your coffee while watching big bold toucans enjoying leftover fruit rinds laid out for them by the cook. Slightly larger than a crow, the toucan has a scimitar-like beak, half the length of its plump body and banded in swaths of red and yellow. Other birds, half the size, which have arrived earlier for a handout, quickly turn tail when the big guys land at the feast.

All of these six Mayan ruins have characteristics in common, but each one has distinctive features as well. At its height of power, 650 AD, Caracol covered one hundred seventy-seven square miles and had a population of possibly one hundred and fifty thousand people. Its scale is grand, and those few excavated structures—of the estimated thirty thousand once in use—are inspiring. By now I've climbed enough steep mossy steps and am satisfied to admire the one hundred and fifty foot high "Sky Palace" from the central Acropolis area.

Our guide for these Mayan sites has been Diana—pronounced Deeana—and a better leader I have never had anywhere, knowledgeable, patient, fun. My friends leave Belize for home rather regretfully, envying me my upcoming week in *Antigua*. There I settle into a comfortable upstairs room at the home of Angelina, and start Spanish language lessons at Probigua Language School. Delightful though my tutor, Julia, is, I am not much of a language student. It's a good thing we have morning classes only. I finally accept the fact that what little I can learn—or relearn—is better than nothing. Don't bother me with grammar, please.

Julia proves helpful to me in an unexpected way. While I'm wandering around *Antigua* alone one afternoon, a temporary crown on a dental implant falls out. Luckily I don't swallow it or lose it, but I don't want to be without that crown for the next six weeks. When I report my problem at the language school, they get me an appointment for the next afternoon, and Julia walks me all over town till we find the dentist's office. His equipment is not as shiny as in this country, but neither is his waiting room as full. It takes Dr. Roberto Vela, wearing no gloves, exactly twenty minutes to re-cement my crown in place and it costs me all of ten dollars.

Volcanoes surround this classical colonial city, and at night one can often see a red ribbon of lava near the top of Vulcan Fuergo. Life in *Antigua* is vibrant, especially as I'm here during Lent. I love sitting in the plaza observing daily life and an occasional religious procession. One day a band is playing "From the Halls of Montezuma" on the steps of the police station. What better place to hang out for a week, hopefully absorbing some Spanish simply by osmosis.

Nicaragua

Speaking of hanging out, that is what I have to do for one very long Sunday at the *Managua* airport when I reach Nicaragua. My TACA flight from *Guatemala City* lands at nine-thirty in the morning, but the volunteer group I am to join, Planting Hope, will not arrive till evening. I've been warned not to wander around *Managua* alone, and since there is no place to check luggage at the airport, that settles it. It's impossible to change money on a Sunday anywhere in Nicaragua, but US dollars work as well as *cordobas*. Since the airport has no restaurant, I subsist on snack food. This enforced day off gets me caught up with my journal entries and some reading.

It still seems a very long time till evening, when Beth and the group from Vermont get in. When it's nearly time for their flight to arrive, a couple of Nicaraguan women who have apparently been observing me, inquire with great solicitude if perhaps I'm in need of a hotel room. I reassure them— touched by their concern—and they direct me to the arrival lounge just as the Continental flight arrives.

Planting Hope is a non-profit that enterprising young Vermonter Beth Merrill established several years ago after spending a semester working near the small city of *Matagalpa*. She has had a library built—Biblioteca La Chispa, or The Spark—and has given support to many other community projects. Our group of sixteen is here to take a good look and help wherever we can, as well as to spread the word about Nicaragua when we get home.

What a diverse group. All Vermonters except me, we range in age from twelve to seventy-eight. There are three families, some enthusiastic teenagers, several teachers, a doctor, and three Sarah's. One is the first person I meet at the airport, another is a nurse, and one of the teenagers is also named Sarah. My niece-in-law, Sandal, has brushed up on her Spanish for this trip, and Darryl speaks it fluently from her days in the Peace Corps in Colombia. But some others have even less of the language than I.

We're all housed with Nicaraguan families in the small town of *San Ramon,* farther up in the hills from *Matagalpa,* north of *Managua.* Widowed Edita is my hard-working hostess. Her household includes two grown sons—Noel and Elmer, daughter-in-law Carolina, who is an Avon saleslady, and young Gabriel, a 3-year old charmer. Among the various homes where our group is housed, I suspect mine may be among the most "rustic." Floors are mostly packed dirt, a single light bulb hangs from each ceiling, and the kitchen is in a back lean-to. Huts for shower and pit toilet are way out back of the house. But of course there is a TV, which is on for long hours each evening.

Edita carefully accompanies me to the *latrina* with her flashlight until I convince her I can manage okay on my own. We can't converse very freely, but I feel safe and well cared for during the week that I am her guest. My narrow room is quite adequate. A candle and yellow flowers provide a tender touch. I awaken early each morning to the sound of chickens, better than the barking dogs that keep some of our group awake at night.

I love to take a pre-breakfast walk every day, in Florida or wherever I happen to be. In foreign countries it's the perfect time to see a community coming to life, to watch the streets being swept, the kids going to school, the shopkeepers opening their doors. Here in this hilly Nicaraguan town it's equally absorbing, especially with the additional pleasure of a fellow walker. I discover that one of the three Sarah's in our group stays at a house around the corner from mine. While walking together every morning, "my" Sarah and I share observations on what we're seeing and doing in our group activities. Two sets of eyes and ears beat one any day. Not surprisingly, we become very good friends in the process.

The meals I am served at Edita's are their family's usual fare—beans and rice, fried plantain, occasionally chicken, and sweet dish-watery coffee. One morning a little old farmer brings Edita a huge bundle of corn husks for which she pays just a few cents. I'm curious, but the next day it all becomes clear, as she gets up extra early and spends the whole day out in the back lean-to kitchen making *tamals*. That evening I find our large side yard converted into an open-air restaurant with *tamals* the entrée. My friend Sarah is invited over, and the two of us are served a fine meal in the house, so I can finally taste *tamals*. Made with a flavorful stuffing of finely ground cornmeal and chicken, they are considered a festive food. They also may contain meat or cheese or almost anything else along with the *masa*.

I've done many volunteer projects in different countries, but this is more of a cultural exchange. Our very full schedule differs each day. We visit schools and community centers, play with the kids, teach the elders card games. The varied talents of our group gradually emerge. Dan's juggling lessons are popular. How many kids now amuse their peers by juggling, I wonder. Origami and craftwork with the students is fun at several schools. Rich plays guitar. Soccer is a hit with all nationalities.

At a rural health center near a school, Dr. Brendan and nurse Sarah from our group assist Dr. Bismarck, the young local medic, in giving shots to youngsters brought here by their mothers from miles away. The doctor and a few of the students get here by horseback. Teachers ride the bus for at least an hour each way and still have to walk a mile or two. Several of us wield purple paint brushes to brighten the *Pueblo Viejo* schoolroom. Vast quantities of donated clothing, which we've brought, get dispersed in a carefully orchestrated "yard sale" in one very poor barrio on the outskirts of *San Ramon*. No money exchanged.

Although we spend limited time at each site, it's our enthusiastic presence that has an impact, I assume, rather than any "work" which is done. Interacting with the people of these impoverished highland communities, even with our limited language skills, is greatly satisfying to all of us. From many in our group I keep hearing the phrase, "a life-changing experience."

All is not work. One hot afternoon we help push our bus down an impossibly pitted road in order to plunge into a waterhole at the base of a glistening waterfall. The icy water is welcome. Later, we watch traditional weaving—and of course buy things—at El Chile, an indigenous weaving school and women's cooperative that Planting Hope sponsors.

Our final weekend is sheer bliss. We all say fond farewells to our host families, and Edita presents me with a broad-brimmed straw hat. Kind, but it's not very packable, so I'm happy to pass it on to one of our gang. I assume that that Nico hat protects against the Vermont sun now.

After a rather dull bus drive south for several hours, we catch a ferry to the beautiful island of Ometepe. Lake Nicaragua seems almost like an ocean, it is so large. In fact, the water rolling in to the shore sounds so much like the sea that you quite expect the water to be salty. But it gives one a cool and refreshing swim, if you can avoid the sharp volcanic stones of the lake bed. What a peaceful place, with Volcano Concepcion to guard over us. I go kayaking with Brendan and Matthew in the jungly lagoon. We could be in the Florida Everglades, except for the loud scary roar of howler monkeys all around us. Here I finally see them lurking in the foliage.

Our final night is in over-rated *Granada.* Then most of our group heads for *Managua* and their flights home, while Rich and I board a comfortable TransNica bus. It's nice to have company as I head south, crossing into Costa Rica an hour later. He gets off farther on to make his way up to beautiful Monteverde Cloud Forest, while I continue to *San Jose.* Watching the farmlands as we pass by, I can't help but notice the dramatic contrast between Nicaragua, the poorest, and Costa Rica, the most prosperous country of Central America.

Costa Rica

Nine hours later I'm in *San Jose,* expecting to see Gail Nystrom, for whom I'll be working during the next couple of weeks. Nobody is at the bus station to meet me, but I wait an hour and make several phone calls, and finally one of her young volunteers arrives to deliver me to my new home stay at Juan and Norma's modern spacious house.

You never know what to expect with a home stay, but they all add to the richness of the experience even if they often test your adaptability. No test is required here; this home is a considerable step up from Edita's in *San Ramon*. I wake up each morning to the aroma of bread baking since Norma is a professional baker, and I'm surrounded by orchids since growing them is Juan's passion. Sons Diego and Daniel and assorted dogs round out the household. Sharp ten-year old Dani recruits me to play cards with him almost every evening.

Unless the boys are around, my conversations with the parents are both tortuous and humorous, a wild mix of Spanish and English, assisted by my constant companion, a pocket Spanish dictionary. Having lived in or visited so many countries in my life has not helped me learn different languages, unfortunately. But it has taught me how many ways there are to communicate. Gestures, mime and sketching are just a few skills that work when you share no common spoken language.

Trim Norma and chatty Juan defy my image of a Latino family. He helps around the house, even washing the pots and pans, and she shows great artistry at decorating elaborate cakes ordered by townspeople, seven on one busy day. Eventually I meet their married daughter and assorted other family members, all very welcoming, some of whom I can talk with in English.

Gail Nystrom is an amazing woman. An American, she has lived in Costa Rica for many years ever since her Peace Corps assignment here hooked her. A single mother, she teaches, writes, and runs almost single-handedly the non-profit "Fundacion Humanitaria" which she established some years ago. Volunteer groups from American universities as well as individuals of all ages come to assist Tico people and organizations in a multitude of ways: paint a mural on an orphanage wall, teach English or computer to low-income kids, build a community center, assist handicapped slum children. Gail sees a need; she finds some way to solve it, whatever it is. You can volunteer for a day or a year; she welcomes you and finds you a Tico household in which to live.

Unlike most of the service organizations I've worked with, it costs very little to volunteer with the Humanitarian Foundation, and in addition you pay a modest amount directly to your home stay host. I am not sure what Gail has in mind for me to do this time. Three years ago my sister Jean and I enjoyed working at a residential rehab center in the little town of *Pozos*. She helped the patients plant a raised garden; I taught yoga.

This year I'm living in the hillside village of *Piedades*, near *Santa Ana*. I'm able to walk each morning to Hogar de Ancienos, a modern home for the elderly where I try to make myself useful. It is run by Catholic nuns and has a spectacular view. Now age seventy-eight, I myself could qualify to live there among the residents who range from sixty-six to one hundred and four. In fact, the oldest of them, a gnome of a man named Chipito, is a regular in our little walking group. A few of us trudge up and down the hilly streets for an hour every morning except when Catholic mass is being said at the home.

Other than that, I'm not given any specific assignments. I help to feed some of the more feeble residents and wander around trying to chat them up—not easy with my rudimentary Spanish—and give a hand with handicrafts. Alain tries to flirt with me—and with any visiting female— but his toothless Spanish is too much for me to decipher. I smile a lot.

This two-and-a-half-week stay in Costa Rica includes almost no time for sightseeing, but I don't mind, as I went to some of the country's volcanoes and national forests three years ago. Still, I have some varied experiences. I join some of the mostly college-age Foundation volunteers at a rural community center a few times to teach the women there how to knit. It's supposed to become an income-producing activity and the women have great fun, but I would not bet on its commercial success. Another day we go to a soup kitchen in *San Jose* to help serve a meal to more than a hundred homeless men, mostly young and very polite. (I do the same thing at the Salvation Army here in Sarasota sometimes.) The manager plays the guitar for hymn singing and leads prayers.

On one most interesting Sunday Gail invites me to go with her to visit two prisons where some of her young Costa Rican protégées are incarcerated and doing well. We join a long line of visitors waiting to pass inspection and enter, but suddenly we are motioned to the head of the line. Gail laughs as she explains that because I'm a senior we get priority. This facility is out in the countryside, and the management seems relatively enlightened if not benign. I think of the huge city prison I visited in *La Paz* and think I'd prefer to serve time in Costa Rica, if that were to be my fate.

Shortly before I pack up and leave their home, Juan asks me if I'll be coming back to Costa Rica. "At my age who knows," I say, and jokingly suggest I might come back and live at the Hogar de Ancienos with the other old folks. They are not amused. Norma emphatically states that No, *this* is my home if I ever want it to be. I am touched. It certainly would make a comfortable abode for much longer than these two weeks, something I cannot say about most of the homes I've stayed at in different countries.

Now it's time to board another bus late one afternoon. These long-distance buses are really comfortable, with TV and air conditioning, on mostly good highways. To get to *San*

Jose from *Granada,* Nicaragua, took nine hours. This trip turns out to be nineteen hours to *Panama City.* I settle in with a book and a stash of bite-sized cream puffs that Norma has pressed upon me for sustenance. What luxury!

Panama

Frontera! Crossing the border into Panama is not the piece of cake we experienced crossing into Costa Rica. Probably being here in the middle of a dark rainy night accentuates my sense of disorientation. Only one man is working the Customs counter and he is far from gracious. Rumors go around among the few *gringos* from our bus that we must show an onward ticket or fork over lots of money. One Israeli couple ends up buying a bus ticket back to *San Jose* which they'll never use, just to satisfy the rules.

After I have wandered on muddy tracks behind huge parked semi trailers to find the counter where I must get a five dollar tourist stamp, I again face the surly Customs officer, almost the last passenger from our bus. With only an E-ticket, how can I prove I am indeed going to depart Panama? Well, I decide to brazen it out, thrusting my unofficial typed itinerary through his little window. He scarcely glances at me, makes a few notes, and doesn't even ask for evidence of my net worth, which had been demanded of the others. Maybe he's ready to call it a day — rather, a night. By this time the border inspectors are ready to close up shop, so I'm not even asked to open my luggage for inspection. This border crossing procedure has taken almost three hours but at last we're underway down the Pan American Highway toward *Panama City.*

To most Americans, Panama means the Panama Canal. This trip opens my eyes to the many other attractions to be found in this snakelike isthmus. We visit national parks to see sloths, monkeys and the elusive Resplendent Quetzal, a spectacular bird. One-fourth of Panama is dedicated to nature preserves. The second largest of these, La Amistad, stretches over the border into Costa Rica. In the lowland city of *David* we spend a couple of hours at the annual fiesta, rather like an American county fair but far more colorful. Next we explore the agricultural Chiriqui Highlands, where the town of *Boquete*, perched on one side of Vulcan Baru, is being invaded by North Americans building retirement homes. Coffee is the biggest crop grown here. But the breakfast coffee we're served is not very good, since top quality coffee gets exported.

Several indigenous peoples are to be found throughout Panama. One highlight is a short flight to spend a night on Dolphin Island, part of the four hundred mile long chain of the San Blas Islands where the semi-autonomous *Kuna* Indians live. Here is where the showy intricate appliqué-work known as *molas* originated. And here is where you have an infinite choice of them if you want to buy a unique example directly from the woman who made it. I do, of course.

Kuna women wear brilliant outfits, with dozens of fine strands of tight-fitting beads on both legs and arms. By contrast, the women of the *Embera* tribe, whom we visit next at their villages alongside the Chagres River, go topless except for a few necklaces looped loosely around their necks. Before going to the islands, I've noticed an occasional *Kuna* woman with her distinctive garb at the airport. But somehow they all seem to resemble each other, or am I seeing the same woman over and over? Once I'm among them on San Blas, I realize that they do indeed share a very strong family resemblance. We're told that that comes from the deliberate attempt to keep their culture pure, which of course leads to intermarriage among the thirty-five thousand people in the tribe. Marrying outside the culture is not forbidden, but it is discouraged. We notice several albino children, another result of this cultural tradition.

We've seen the Panama Canal from several vantage points, but now we're going to make a partial transit of it on the final day of our tour. Our boatload of tourists is not big enough to go through the locks alone, so a huge container ship, the Cap Sarcy, follows behind us, too close for comfort at times. Of the three sets of locks along the fifty-mile-long canal, we transit two, heading south from *Gamboa* towards the capital. Amazing though it is to see the walls of the locks rise above us as we're being lowered, much of this day is pretty tedious. We make our way under the new Centennial Bridge, almost a replica of Tampa Bay's beautiful Sunshine Skyway Bridge, and through the Gaillard Cut at the Continental Divide. I've heard friends say that they would only want to make a *full* transit of the canal, but after almost five hours aboard our vessel, I'm delighted that we're not doing the whole thing.

In fact, I'm ready to head home to my own welcoming *Sarasota* nest, even though there are a couple of nearby countries I've missed. I figure I've slept in some twenty different beds during my eight weeks of travel, three of them in local households. So many Central American people are arriving in Florida daily that I'm glad to have experienced a taste of what life is like not so far south of the border. *Hasta Luego!*

AFTERWORD

Do I still travel the same way these days? Well, yes and no. After renting out my condo for the winter months for some thirteen years, enabling me to travel economically, I had a sudden epiphany when I got home in 2005. Weary from eight weeks on the go in six Central American countries, I was unpacking when the thought hit me: "You don't *have* to keep doing this. It was your own idea and it has worked very well, but nobody's forcing you to keep doing it forever." Suddenly, I felt wonderfully free.

I haven't stopped traveling, not by a long shot, but I'm no longer locked into a precise time of year and length of journey. As it happens, I had no sooner absorbed this new state of mind than I had an invitation to join friends going to Turkey the following April. On my normal schedule that would have been impossible, but under the new open calendar I accepted eagerly, and even added on two weeks in Egypt, not returning home till early May.

Later that year, I received a fabulous invitation to accompany my special friend John on a November trip starting in Portugal and crossing the Atlantic westward to Antigua on the Sea Cloud II. Again, had I been gearing up for a long winter's journey, how could I have participated in that splendid and unusual sailing expedition? It just illustrates how great I find it nowadays to go away for any length of time and at any time of the year, cost being the only constraint. Preparing my space for winter renters didn't seem difficult during those thirteen years, but now that I don't have to do it, I realize how much more carefree my packing up has become.

People have the impression that you must be wealthy to travel, but it's all a matter of priorities. Do you want a new car every few years, or would you rather see the world? I live simply; I travel frugally. I usually choose places where I get good value, where my dollars stretch. Many of my favorite locales are in developing countries, where one would not want to appear extravagant, but where there are grand adventures to be had.

Right now I'm preparing for a tour in Brazil, Argentina and Chile. My friends think I've been everywhere, but of course that's not true. I don't keep count, but it must be some sixty-five countries that I've at least peeked at, on six different continents. Some travelers so love the first country they visit that they keep returning there exclusively. I have more curiosity. Although I often return to favorite spots, I also need the exhilaration of new vistas. There's still a lot of world out there, and I intend to keep exploring it for as long as my wallet and my energy permit. When that is no longer possible, I have a trunk full of travel slides with which to relive my far-ranging journeys. Armchair travel may have to satisfy this great appetite for far places. I've taken lots of people on vicarious adventures that way over the years. Maybe someone else will do that for me when my wings have been clipped by some unforeseen circumstance that puts "Stop" to my fantastic life as a voyager.

Meanwhile, what horizons beckon next? How about Ecuador, Crete, Madagascar, maybe Mongolia?